FIXED LIVES

FIXED LIVES

TRUE LIFE CHANGING STORIES FROM THE WORLD OF ADDICTION

proclaimtrust

malcolm down

PUBLISHING

CONTENTS

FOREWORD BY J.JOHN

There are two potential kinds of readers for this remarkable book: those who are in the grip of addiction and those who are not.

If you are someone who has an addiction problem, then why not skip the rest of this foreword and simply start reading these accounts? Here, written in plain, honest language you will find remarkable testimonies of men and women who have been set free by Jesus Christ from the power of drug addiction. And here we are talking permanently free. No one involved in any form of addiction finds the one-liner, 'Anyone can give up drugs, I've done it a dozen times' remotely funny. Those with 'substance problems' know only too well how addiction comes to have a seemingly unbreakable grip on your life. Yet the stories here are of men and women who have been set free and whose lives have indeed been *fixed* to the extent that they are now able to hold down useful jobs, have a fulfilled family life and play a valuable part in society. Read this thoughtfully, read this prayerfully: there is hope for you here.

Now, if you aren't in the grip of an addiction then let me commend this book to you for three reasons.

First, this book is an encouragement to a deep gratitude. It is reported that on seeing a line of people being led to execution, the sixteenth-century Christian leader John

Bradford commented, 'There but for the grace of God goes John Bradford.' That is a wise and sensible attitude. In this book you get a chilling and enduring impression of the power and misery of addiction. It's easy to say to ourselves that we would never get into drugs and that, if we did, we would be able to break free through our own determination and strength of will. The truth is otherwise; drugs and alcohol have enslaved and ruined better and stronger men and women than you or me. Our reaction on reading these accounts should indeed be, 'There but for the grace of God go I.'

Now, gratitude is a good thing and if you're not a Christian, it can be the first step to faith. After all, you need someone to give thanks to. Try it! And if you are a Christian, you need to be reminded that thanksgiving is something that should be part and parcel of your daily existence. Too often prayer is about asking God for blessings we would like to have rather than thanking him for the blessings we have already been given. Read this book and give thanks!

Second, this book is an encouragement to a real faith. We sometimes get the impression that our culture offers the Christian believer only two choices: to have a faith or not to have one. That is misleading and dangerous. In reality there is a third option: the temptation to hold a watered-down version of Christianity. This 'Christianity-lite' is a gentle, inoffensive, private religion that focuses on a modest morality wrapped up in fine words. It's a religion that is universally acceptable – there's nothing in it to give offence – and poses no threat to our career prospects, our friendships or our social standing. It is a quiet and largely invisible religion that is unlikely to cause any personal difficulties or embarrassment. Yet this popular but anaemic version of the real thing isn't the religion of the Bible. And it certainly isn't a faith that saves men and women from the depths of despair.

To read this book is to come face to face – perhaps uncomfortably – with a lively, vigorous, full-strength faith in Christ: a religion of power, miracles and changed lives. Notice in reading these accounts that these are people who, in most cases, have had the benefit of every treatment and discipline our world can offer them: rehabilitation programmes, chemical substitutes, counselling programmes and even jail sentences. These things have achieved little or nothing, yet, where they have failed, Jesus Christ has succeeded. The world does not need another religion, even if it takes the name of Christianity. What it does need is a vital and supernatural faith in a living Christ who operates today in the power of his Spirit and who can set men and women free from all that binds them. If you are not a Christian, read these accounts and have your absence of faith challenged. If you are a Christian, read them and find the quality of your faith challenged.

Finally, this book is an encouragement to a genuine compassion. We live in times when lip service is paid to the care and rehabilitation of those who suffer from substance abuse. There are, we are confidently told, programmes and schemes to deal with such people. Thus reassured, we feel able to turn our backs on them. Yes, we say, we are concerned about problems of addiction, but in truth our concerns are no more than getting such people off our streets and out of sight. To read this book is to be reminded that addicts are not some separate species whose plight we can ignore, but rather real people with hopes, fears and loves like ours. In these bald accounts, devoid of sentimentalism and dramatisation, we see the heartbreaking tragedy of those trapped in the world of drugs. We should have our hearts moved.

Yet to read this book is not simply to hear about those people who have been rescued from addiction – it is to be reminded of those who helped them on the way out. In that costly rescuing we see a faith which combines proclaiming Jesus in words with living out a relationship with him in deeds. This is the gospel faith at its best and most authentic.

This is a challenging book that asks us all probing questions. Am I thankful for the blessings I have received from God and for the perils from which I have been spared? Do I know anything of this Spirit-empowered Christian faith that believes that even the most desperate of lives can be changed by God? Perhaps, above all, it asks what I am doing to help those who have fallen into the trap of addiction. Read and be encouraged! Read and be challenged!

J.John, author and speaker.

INTRODUCTION

I was a heroin addict for fifteen years. In 1996 a sequence of extraordinary circumstances changed my life forever. My life was FIXED. Subsequently, I founded a charity called Proclaim Trust.

In 2013, Proclaim Trust hosted the first FIXED Conference. This conference was geared towards ex-addicts, recovering addicts, addicts and those with a heart for addicts. It was the first conference of its kind, with hundreds of attendants from all over the United Kingdom.

We didn't realise at the time that the conference would become an annual fixture, reaching more people affected by addiction each year.

Addiction affects so many individuals worldwide – broken people searching for a way to get FIXED.

Fixed Lives, the book, is a collection of stories about people who were once caught up in the cycle of addiction. I consider all the contributors to *Fixed Lives* my personal friends. *Fixed Lives* provides intriguing and sometimes shocking insights into these individuals' lives; real lives that have been totally changed. Their lives have been FIXED.

Barry Woodward
Proclaim Trust

I. ADELLE HOWELLS

It was January 2013 and I'd just started a course through the job centre. It was on that course that I met a girl called Jo. I became really good friends with Jo, and after the course had finished we kept in touch, going round to each other's houses for tea and meeting in town for coffee. The more I got to know her the more I opened up, and I started to tell her about things that had happened in my life, and how both my parents were addicts. Then, one day in March, as we were chatting, Jo told me about a conference called Fixed which was run by a guy called Barry Woodward who heads up an organisation called Proclaim Trust.

Jo told me this conference was for ex-addicts, recovering addicts, addicts, or those with a heart for addicts, and there'd be some seminars for people with addiction or those working with people who were addicted. This was only a few days before the conference was about to happen, but knowing about my background and the kind of life I'd lived, Jo decided she would ask me if I wanted to go. I didn't really know where I fitted into this conference, but I really felt that I needed to attend. I guess I thought it might help me understand the world of addiction from a different perspective. Jo knew that I really wanted to get involved in helping people who had been affected by family members who were addicts, because that was the kind of lifestyle I had, growing up.

Jo said to me, 'If you want, you can come with me. Just message Barry on Facebook, tell him you're a friend of mine, and say you would like to come with me.'

'OK, I will!' I said.

Jo said she would message Barry too.

Then she told me that this conference was going to be at a church, and I remember thinking: 'Great . . . I don't do church! I'm just not into all that "God Squad" stuff.' I should have known, really, with her always going on about being a Christian! I thought to myself, 'Church might be for her, but it's not for me.' But the more I thought about it, the more I felt I needed to go. So just a few days before the conference, I messaged Barry and told him about my background, and how I felt what I had been through must have been for a reason, and so I was searching for a way to use my past experiences for good. I then asked if it would be OK for me to go to Fixed.

Barry replied and said, 'Yes, of course you can come to Fixed! Just turn up with Jo.'

I found out later that I was actually the last person to book into Fixed, and it completely changed my life.

One of my earliest memories is from when I was five years old. We were living in a terraced house on Langshaw Street in Old Trafford. I walked into the kitchen one day to find my mum on the floor going cold turkey – she was withdrawing from heroin, and all I could think about was finding her medicine (that's what I called it back then). If I could find that then I could make my mum better. You see, I am the child an addict.

I started my first primary school in Old Trafford, Seymour Park Primary School. I had no idea back then, but that school was going to be the first of thirteen different schools I'd end up going to.

Growing up, I didn't think my life was any different to anyone else's. But once I reached the age of about ten and we were living in Radcliffe, Greater Manchester, I realised it was different to my friends' lives, and my mum was actually an addict. I'd overhear conversations between my mum and her friends about scoring; they'd all be talking about getting 'a white and a b', and then they would send me to the shop for tinfoil. I always got to keep the change for some sweets, so I didn't mind going to the shop.

My dad was an addict too, but I didn't know this till I was older. He didn't live with us because my parents had split up before I was born. He would come and visit me from time to time – until eventually he just stopped coming.

When Mum and I were living in Radcliffe, drugs, alcohol and violence were on the scene a lot, so I'd just go out to get out of the way. I hated being at home when it was all kicking off.

One time, when I was about eleven years old, I got myself into a fight with a boy from my class at school. During this time I was being sexually abused on a regular basis by someone me and my mum knew very well – I was best friends with his daughter at the time and I used to stay at her house a lot – but I never told anyone; I just kept it to myself. I became angry and just wanted to lash out and so I got arrested for the first time ever and charged with ABH (Actual Bodily Harm). There I was, getting out of the house to get away from the violence, and now I was becoming violent myself. Home life was having an impact on me that I never even realised.

I started high school in Radcliffe. I tried my first cigarette there too, round the back of the sports hall. I choked on the first drag and wondered why on earth people would enjoy smoking and decided I wasn't going to do that, but then a few months later I tried again and it was better; I didn't choke this time and I started to enjoy it.

During my first year at Radcliffe High there was a lot going on at home, but I never spoke about it at school until one day when I was pulled out of a lesson to be told that someone from social services had come to speak to me. My heart sank and it took me right back to the time my mum left me with Bury social services.

We were living in Bury, again in Greater Manchester, at my mum's boyfriend's place at the time. He was called John. He was about six foot tall, skinny as a rake, and always had this really angry look on his face. His house was dark because he never opened the curtains, and there was always weed and money lying around the place. He had a German Shepherd dog called Bow that would always cower when John raised his voice. I hated John. He and my mum would always be arguing and fighting, and my mum would always end up worse off. I was so sick of having to live like this; I thought it was better when Mum and I were on our own. So one day I was in the house on my own – John had gone away for a few days and Mum had nipped out. I decided I was going to set fire to his house. I left the electric cooker on and put a pile of paper on the hobs. Then I took Bow and left the house.

My plan didn't go as well as I would have liked, though, because my mum came back a while later and put the fire out. A few days after that, when John came home, there was another massive argument. Then Mum took me into Bury town centre. That's when she started asking me all these questions, like:

'Would you not like to live with another family in a nice home, Dell?'

'Do you not think it would be nice to have a break from me for a while?'

'Maybe it would be better if you stayed with someone else for a bit?'

I didn't really understand what she was saying or why she was asking me all these questions until we were walking through the doors of Bury social services.

As soon as I knew what was happening I tried to run away, but a lady social worker wrapped both her arms around me and just held me there as I watched my mum walk away. You know what? My mum never looked back once. I was screaming for her to come back, but she just kept walking. I struggled so much to get to my mum that I ended up ripping open the social worker's blouse, and still she didn't let me go.

My mum had left me, and that was a day I would never forget. I was heartbroken. Now I was with a bunch of strangers who were telling me I wasn't going to see my mum for a while, but they would take me to stay with a nice family.

I didn't know it then, but the argument my mum had had with John had left Mum and I with nowhere to live, and my mum had no choice but to put me in care temporarily. All I knew was that my mum had left me, and I felt so abandoned. You can imagine what I must have been thinking when I was faced with the social services for a second time while I was at school.

Mum had got herself into another violent relationship and things weren't going well at all. She decided it was time to leave, but this time I was given a choice: I could stay there at that school and go into care, or I could leave and go with my mum. Well, there was no way I was going back into care again, so I chose to go with my mum, and we moved into a hostel in Rochdale.

I was twelve years old when we moved into the hostel, and I was now at my twelfth school. Stability wasn't something I was used to. I was getting good at making new friends and getting used to new environments.

I was well into smoking by now, drinking at the weekends and smoking weed. At the age of fourteen I ended up pregnant by someone who was much older than me. I wasn't naïve about sex because by the time I was twelve I had been sexually abused for over twelve months. It took away my innocence and opened my eyes to a world I shouldn't have known anything about. So, by the time I was fifteen I was smoking weed daily and had become a teenage mum.

My son's dad was called Andy and I had met him through some friends of mine. He lived just round the corner from my school, so my friends and I used to go to his house to smoke weed. I got quite friendly with Andy and I started going there on my own. We got on really well and he made me feel like I could just be myself.

Then I started going to Andy's more and more. I would go to his place when things were tough at home, and he would listen to me and cheer me up. We had some laughs, me and Andy.

It wasn't that long after I started going to Andy's that I had a bust-up with my mum. I'd become an angry teenager, blaming my mum and her drug habit – and, at that time, drinking problem – for everything. So I ended up leaving home. I was staying at a friend's house who I used to babysit for, so now and then if it got a bit late I would sleep over at Andy's. Nothing ever happened between me and Andy until one night, one thing led to another, and I ended up sleeping with him. I got pregnant just two weeks before my fifteenth birthday.

I remember sitting in the clinic waiting to have my pregnancy test, thinking I was wasting my time. Then the nurse called me into the room and she took my sample away to be tested. She came back and said, 'The test is positive.'

I said, 'What?'

She said, 'The test is definitely positive; you are pregnant.'

I was in complete shock. No way did I think I would end up pregnant.

I remember coming home from the hospital with my brand-new baby boy. He was so small, only 5lb 1oz, his head was shiny, bald, and his skin was almost transparent. I put him down on the changing mat in front of me, and as I faced him for the first time at home on my own, I thought, 'Oh no, what have I done? What am I gonna do? How am I gonna cope?' There I was, fifteen years old – I was a child with a child of my own. This tiny little baby boy was now dependent on me for absolutely everything, and I had no idea how I was going to cope.

On my sixteenth birthday, I was given the keys to my first ever home. It was a three-bedroomed flat on a rundown housing estate called Falinge. I used to hang around on the Falinge estate before I got pregnant, so I knew the area well, and it was just down the road from Andy's.

The day I was handed the keys to my first-ever home on this deprived estate, I had no money, no furniture, and a three-month-old baby to look after. Suddenly my journey had become very hard. And who would have believed it? By the time I was seventeen years old I was back in the very same hostel I was in with my mum just a few years before. But this time I was there with my own child, and for the same reason my mum was there – fleeing from a violent relationship. I started to realise I was following in my mum's footsteps, and had even started taking other drugs, like speed and ecstasy. I also dabbled in a bit of cocaine.

When I left that hostel I got my own place. I moved a couple of times after that, then eventually settled on estate called Newbold. By this point in my life I had not seen my dad for nine years, but through my auntie I had got back in touch with him. He had left his phone number with her for me to contact him, so I rang him and he started to come to see me. I used to think he was coming to spend time with me, but in truth, I never really got much time with him when he visited, because he spent more time with my mum, getting high on drugs, mostly crack and heroin.

One night while my dad was staying at my place he asked me to go out and score some drugs for him. My dad was a heroin addict, but he couldn't get hold of any heroin so he asked me to score him some phet (amphetamine). This wasn't out of the ordinary with parents like mine, and my dad knew that I knew where to get it from, because at the time I was taking it myself. I didn't want to go, though, because I had been up partying the previous two nights, and all I wanted was to go to bed. But he just kept on at me, so eventually I went out and got it for him.

Later that night my dad took those drugs and they triggered a brain haemorrhage. I thought he just had a bit of a headache so I went to bed and left him to go to sleep on the couch. I came downstairs the next morning with my son to give him his breakfast, and I went into the front room to find my dad dead on the floor.

I didn't realise he was dead at first. I wondered why he was lying on the floor and not on the couch, so I tapped his foot with mine to wake him up, and that's when I felt a cold shiver down my spine. I looked at him and his face was grey. I've never been so scared in my life. The drugs I'd gone out and got for him had killed him. Can you imagine how I felt?

Death by misadventure, they called it. That was the worst experience of my life and I was consumed with guilt.

Nine years on, I was still consumed with guilt. By now I had two children and was living on my own. That's when I met Jo and she invited me to Fixed. From that day my life completely changed.

When I walked into that conference in 2013, it wasn't at all what I had thought. I wasn't expecting church to look like that! There were no wooden seats and no stained-glass windows! It was really modern. I remember looking round at everyone and thinking, 'All these people look like my mum's friends!' and to be honest, I was half-expecting one of them to walk through the door.

That conference blew me away – the atmosphere, the music, the speakers. Many times during that day there were opportunities for me to respond to Jesus, and every time I felt as though God was speaking to me, but I just didn't move. I argued with myself for ages, then I looked at Jo.

'Will they be doing that again?' I asked.

'Doing what?' she said.

'You know, that thing!' I said.

She looked at me. 'No, Dell, I don't know what you mean! What thing?'

I could tell her patience was wearing thin because her face could never hide what she was thinking. So I just came out with it: 'That thing where they can say that prayer and ask God into their lives.'

Suddenly her face changed and she said, 'Oh yeah, of course they will. Why? Do you want to . . .?'

I butted straight in. 'No! I was just asking, that's all!'

I kept listening to these speakers, and it was as if God was talking directly to me through what they were saying, and still I didn't move.

Then, in the evening, Barry Woodward got up to speak. That's when I heard about Jesus; that's when I heard how he paid the price for all our faults, flaws and failures, and that no matter what we had done we could be forgiven. I sat back in my seat and remember thinking, 'Wow! So what he is saying is that I can be forgiven for what happened to my dad. I don't need to carry this guilt any more.'

Before I knew it, Barry was at the end of his talk, and then he invited people to say a prayer. Inside I was shaking; my emotions were all over the place. I needed to do this! Everybody stood up and bowed their heads and prayed the prayer together, including me. Then Barry invited those who had said that prayer for the first time to come to the front. I flew from my seat and straight to the front before Jo could even blink! It was then that I felt the guilt I'd lived with for years just lift straight off me. I was so relieved, and then I was filled with this amazing feeling of love. I'd been searching for this feeling of love all my life. I'd been looking for it in drugs, in relationships, in all kinds of things, but I'd never felt it until that evening. It was there on 23 March 2013 that I became a Christian. I knew from that moment things were never going to be the same.

The following week, still filled with this amazing feeling, I decided I would go to church. So I went to Kirkholt Community Church in Rochdale, because that's where Jo went. From the minute I walked into that church I was welcomed with open arms. They supported me so much, and I did some courses with them that helped me discover all about my new life as a Christian. On 22 September, just six months after the Fixed conference, I was baptised at my church. Being baptised was incredible; better than any drug I had taken! It was a new high I'd never experienced before.

I'm now proud to say that I am totally into all that 'God Squad' stuff! I'm very much involved in my church.

A few months after Fixed, I messaged Barry, telling him

how grateful I was that I was able to go to Fixed and that I was now going to church. We arranged to meet up for a chat at a friend's house. I took the certificates I'd got from the courses I had done at my church. While I was chatting with Barry, I told him how I knew my life couldn't have been the way it was for nothing, and I wanted to use those experiences to help others. Barry was really encouraged by how far I had come since Fixed, and a few months later asked me if I would like to do some voluntary work at the Trust.

So in January 2014 I started working as a volunteer for Barry at Proclaim Trust. In the beginning I was just doing a couple of hours each week, then in the June I became a paid administrator and am now Barry's PA.

One of my main roles since starting at the Trust is to work alongside Barry in organising the Fixed conference. It's such an honour to be able to organise the conference that changed my life and where I became a Christian. Even more amazingly, in October 2014 I was privileged to speak at Fixed and to share my story with around 500 people. Then, in November, I got married to my husband, Brad, who is actually my pastor's son – so now my pastor is my father-in-law! God has blessed me more than I could have ever imagined.

I've now realised through working for the Trust that I have found my purpose in life. I'm an evangelist with a story to tell that can help others and give them hope.

2. PAUL LLOYD

I'll never forget the day my life took a completely different turn. It was 1995. Blackburn Rovers had won the Premiership title, which I cared nothing about, me being a West Ham supporter. John Major was having a tricky time as Prime Minister, I'd just celebrated my twenty-seventh birthday . . . and my life was about to change in a way I would never have expected.

It was a hot Tuesday evening in July in the East End of London, with that uncomfortable stickiness that people always seem to moan about. I was definitely uncomfortable. I had just had my life threatened by a drug dealer that I didn't even know, due to a mad situation with a girl I was seeing, and I was driving myself crazy trying to work out what I should do about it. These things were part and parcel of the life I was living. I was a drug dealer, and (when necessary) a violent criminal.

My twelve years of drug abuse had reduced my once-fit, combat-trained body down to a shell of grey skin with needle scars up my arms and hands and neck. The news of what this other random lunatic was saying he was going to do to me had filtered through from my girlfriend's mate and now I was driving around, sweating, with my brain boiling with options. I could just leave it and hope it was only big talk – but that generally ended up badly with other sharks smelling blood in the water and coming to have a bite – or I could 'make a statement'. I knew how to do that; after all, I'd survived for over a decade on the streets of East London, and you don't do that without learning a few tricks and making a few statements. And I knew how to get it done right – meaning, not get caught for it. The best way to do that was to do it alone, because unless you were very stupid, you wouldn't grass yourself up!

But for some reason, I found myself driving to see one of my oldest and closest friends for help. Dee was a few years older than me, but we'd always been close growing up. He was a good friend to have – very switched-on, a moneymaker, ex-prizefighter, and a very dangerous criminal who had somehow slipped into the world of money broking in the City of London. This turned out to be a great opportunity for me, as I was able to serve up huge amounts of cocaine and cannabis to his colleagues.

Our addictions grew worse together, but as we were living in different worlds now, we tended to only see each other when he wanted me to arrange a big parcel for one of his pals, so we hadn't seen each other for a good while. In fact, I hadn't seen him since the funeral of one of my other good mates, Neil, who had died of a heroin overdose.

If you were to ask me why I found myself outside his door that night, I honestly wouldn't be able to tell you. Sure, we'd done things like this together before and I trusted him, but he'd become legit, which changes things. Maybe I knew I was too messed-up now to be confident of pulling off something as dangerous as the thing I was planning to do on my own, and was hoping for back-up. After all, since my teenage street gang days, when we were out to make our mark, and then my early criminal career when I was part of a fully fledged, up-and-coming criminal enterprise made up of young, dangerous men looking to emulate the older gangsters, I had been doing things increasingly on my own. Addiction takes you that way. And it's tiring. Maybe that was it? I wanted a bit of help to carry the weight of it? I don't know, but there I was. I knocked on the door, it opened, and Dee stood there smiling. Only he looked different – unusually happy – like he'd just won the Lottery or had taken a particularly good ecstasy tablet.

''Ello, mate,' Dee said in his strong Cockney accent. 'Come in. Whass 'appenin'? I ain't seen you in a while. Sit down and I'll stick the kettle on. 'Ow's yer ole man?'

In my mind I was thinking that he must be off his head on some really crazy designer drug, because he was just too chirpy. Maybe this was a bad idea?

When he finally sat down, I told him about my bit of drama and then dropped the nugget about what I was thinking of doing. And while he thought about it, I thought I'd sweeten things up.

'Fancy a cheeky bit of gear?' I said, while pulling out a ball of heroin and my 'works' – which consisted of a well-burned tablespoon, some insulin syringes and some vitamin C powder. I placed everything on the table and waited for Dee to jump in.

'Sorry mate, I can't help ya. And I don't do gear anymore. I've become a Christian!'

A Christian? Dee?! What did that mean? What was going on here? This was all a bit surreal, especially as he started launching into what had happened to him and what the Bible said about this and that and the other.

'Hold up! What? You've done what?' I couldn't wrap my head around it. 'You gonna start wearing sandals and doing jumble sales?' I said, laughing. 'I've got a bit of drama here with this other fella, and you're waffling on like you're about to star on *Songs of Praise*. Sort it out. This is serious!'

That was it. He was off again. Now, I'd always believed in God. I'd even prayed before. But here was my good mate talking as if he knew God – like he was a pal.

'Right. Nice one, Dee. I'm gonna have to go 'cos you're doing my head in.'

'Paul, where you gonna go when you die?'

That was the final straw. 'Look, I'm not a nonce (paedophile) and I'm not a grass. I'm not evil, and we both know a few bods that are. So I'll probably go to heaven, mate. I believe in God.'

'Well, the Bible says that none of us are good enough to go to heaven in our own strength. Look at some of the things we've done. If you're not careful, the way you're living, you'll end up like Neil and Bolts and Crocko. All dead. That's why we need Jesus. 'Cos he paid the price for our madness, and if we believe in him and turn from our old ways, to him, he'll forgive us and save our souls and make us new – and he can even get you off the gear!'

'Dee, God don't want me in his squad. I'm too bad to be "saved"! I've broke all the Ten Commandments. I'm a junkie. This is it, mate!'

'Paul, Jesus didn't come for the well – he came for the sick. That's what you are. Mate, Jesus wants you. Why don't you come to the gym tomorrow and we can talk more?'

'Maybe I will. Anyway, later,' I said as I made a quick exit with my mind completely mangled. Forgetting my other bit of drama, I went home and spent the rest of the night in a sweaty, drugged-out stupor.

Wednesday night was another hot one. I'd slipped about all day keeping my head down, because you never knew if the next motorbike was going to be carrying a nasty person with a gun. It was a quiet day, as I didn't need to drop any drugs off anywhere or pick up any money, so once again I found myself on the way to somewhere and couldn't tell you why. Was I curious about the things Dee had told me? I think I probably was. I definitely didn't want to be a junkie anymore. That had never been my intention in the beginning. It just sort of crept up on me like a sneaky addiction ninja. And then I was stuck on the self-destruction treadmill, going downhill and losing more than I made. And I made a lot of money – probably enough to be comfortable for the rest of my days – if I hadn't lived like a waster; drugs, drink, women, clothes, and hot countries.

So when I walked into the gym, I had no idea what I was in for. Both Dee and the gym owner, an old friend, had become Christians. They told me about their experiences and gave me Bible verses to back them up. I kept telling them I was too far gone. But as I got up to leave, one of them said, 'Paul, what have you got to lose?'

That stopped me for a minute. Something shifted.

They gave me a little card with a prayer written on it – 'the sinner's prayer', where you surrender your life to Jesus, confessing you believe he died on the cross, taking the punishment for everything we have ever said or done to hurt God and other people, and that he rose from the dead and is alive today. You ask him to take over your life, and as I walked out the last thing I remember was being encouraged to pray.

As I sat in my car those words, 'What have you got to lose?' kept going round in my head. So I took a breath and said the words on the card . . . and nothing happened!

But then I closed my eyes and spoke out loud.

'God, if you're real, and I believe you are; if what they've said about Jesus is true, and if you will forgive me and break my addiction, I'll serve you forever!'

Suddenly I knew that my life was going to be different. My eyes grew wet and tears began to run down my face. I was still an addict, but I just knew deep down that something had changed and I was going to be free.

That was the beginning of my new life. I struggled at first; I was a Christian with a heroin addiction. But the difference was that now I had hope. I began attending a Full Gospel Church in Dagenham called Bethel. I was baptised there in October 1995 and very soon started attending meetings held by a couple of people who were working for Teen Challenge. They had a dream of starting a centre in East London, and went out on the streets in an old single-decker bus telling people about Jesus. I went with them – to the very places that I used to sell drugs. But as much as I tried, my addiction wasn't fully broken. I knew Jesus could do it, but I'd slip back in. I even decided to go into the Teen Challenge centre in Wales, but couldn't get a place, even though I was hanging about with their representatives in the East End.

In the midst of this battle, something amazing happened. My dad became a Christian. I took him with me to a Christmas Eve meeting at Bethel and he made his own commitment to Jesus, and has been serving at that same church ever since.

I also had my first encounter with the supernatural Word of God. My friend had got saved – another lunatic! – and Dee and I had given him a book called *Addicted* (Now republished as *Out of the Ruins,* 2016), written by a pastor called Steve Derbyshire. We decided to go and meet Steve, so off we went on a mission to find him. We went to his church, City Gates, in Ilford, East London. The caretaker told us he would be at his offices, so we walked in asking for him. In hindsight we must've caused a bit of a disruption – three aggressive-looking men with scars and tattoos loudly asking, 'Where's Steve?'

Pastor Steve came out and, after a moment of silence, we explained the situation and asked him to pray for our mate, Peter, which he did. But suddenly, in the middle of the prayer, he stopped and said that God didn't usually do this, but had given him a clear message for someone. And he pointed straight at me. He began to say that God was going to use me as a leader and to preach to thousands of people of different nationalities, and that I would communicate to them in ways they would understand. Then he finished and with a few laughs and slaps on the back we left – me with my head completely mangled, as I'd been told all this amazing stuff but was still struggling with heroin.

But then in 1996 someone told me about Victory Outreach

– a church that had a facility for people coming from addiction. They called a place called 'The Home' based in Holloway, North London, with the actual church located in East London. I went there and had an interview and agreed to enter the programme the very next day. That's what I needed – immediate help. So I found myself on a Friday night on The Highway in Wapping, East London, walking from Tower Hill tube station with my little bag of clothes and toiletries, heading for the Victory Outreach London church service. I had a bag of heroin and knew that I was about to go into a no-drug place, so I smoked it in the toilet of a petrol station near the church. That was the last time I ever used heroin. As I went up to the door of the church, I stubbed out the last cigarette I'd ever smoke, and walked into the adventure of a lifetime. I'd made my mind up to stay for two weeks with these full-on nutters, then I'd go back to my manor and live happily ever after. That was twenty years ago!

Victory Outreach Recovery Homes are incredible places. They differ throughout the world due to different personalities and cultures, but the expectation is fundamentally the same throughout – you come in as an addict and leave as a man or woman of God. That essential transformation comes through getting to know Jesus. Sure, there are courses that you go on and teachings that are practical and necessary, but I'd been on those before. For me it was the times of prayer and worship, and Bible study with people from my background who'd had similar experiences that turned me inside out and upside down. The church people also played their part. We had families and business people, builders and doctors, and the pastor was a geologist! All sorts of nationalities and backgrounds came together to reach and help people like me.

I was filled with the Holy Spirit and received an understanding of why I was alive and what I could do with my life. I was in the programme for nine months, and during that time went on missions to India, where I stayed in the Recovery Home in Madras, and where I witnessed biblical-level miracles, to Scotland, Ireland, Europe and America. I met ex-gangsters, ex-Mafia – both Italian and Mexican – ex-junkies and former alcoholics and jailbirds. The stories would swing between having you cracking up with laughter to stories of abuse and madness that would have you weeping. But through it all, the change that I went through from the inside-out was real and has to be experienced to be fully appreciated. You come to the understanding that your past is not a life sentence, but a lesson to learn from.

It was rarely easy and there were many times I considered leaving – and a few times I considered GBH – but I remembered where I'd come from, and just kept putting one spiritual foot in front of the other. Eventually, I was leading the other men in a position of trust and responsibility, and then I graduated from the programme. I was given the sobering news that I hadn't made it yet, but that my journey was just beginning, now as a man free from that old lifestyle.

I walked into the reality of a world that I'd been numb to for many years. It was the year that Prince Charles and Princess Diana divorced. The IRA were still causing havoc and had bombed the Docklands and the centre of Manchester. I was free, I was clean and I was on a mission. I moved into a flat in Camden Town with another couple of graduates. We were involved in everything that had to do with church. We'd work during the day and then be on the streets or in a service at night. It might sound a bit much, but we were grateful and loved it.

To show how real it all was, we were having some central heating fitted and I moved a wardrobe in my bedroom. Sitting right there on the floor were two bags of heroin. How is that possible? The previous occupants of the flat had been dealers, we subsequently found out. Both bags went down the toilet. My life had changed.

I moved from there to oversee a Victory Outreach second phase house – a place where those about to graduate go to live for around three to four months – in Kennington, South London, and then was asked to go to Israel in early 1999 to help start a Recovery Home with a VO pastor from New York. What a privilege! What an adventure!

I returned late in 1999 to become part of the pastoral staff of the VO London church, where I led the outreach and trained Recovery Home directors. All this time I was studying because I believed that this was my focus now. I was working in construction by day to pay for my mission trips and the international conferences I was attending, and at night I was involved in reaching and helping people who were like I used to be. Then in 2000 I took my Ministerial Credential exam and passed. In five years I'd gone from being a violent, hopeless drug dealer and addict, to becoming a reverend! Only Jesus could pull that off.

In that same year, a lovely looking woman entered our

Women's Recovery Home. She was also a long-time addict, but there was something about her; she wanted the same things I did. She also graduated from the programme. And on 5 October 2002, in a ceremony at a beautiful country house in Ongar, Essex, that had a few people in attendance shedding some tears, we were married. We moved into a one-bed, no central heating, hovel of a flat on Woodberry Down estate in Hackney . . . but we loved it. We had very little money, as prior to our wedding I'd been living in one of our Recovery Homes in Leytonstone while training a new director, and to be really honest, there's not much money in Christian drug recovery! But as we like to say: 'We're not in it for the income. We're in it for the outcome.'

Little did we know that events would transpire in such a way that exactly one year later – actually, on our first wedding anniversary! – we'd be installed as pastors of the Victory Outreach Manchester church. There were seventeen people in attendance, and ten were there for us from London.

That day in 2003 was the start of another mad adventure – one that would have major lows and amazing highs. A journey through laughter and tears, miscarriage, and the joy of children, cancer and sickness and accidents, and the joy of healing; financial hardship and miraculous provision – to miracles of changed lives and the growth of a church that is taking its place in the pivotal city that Manchester is becoming in the history of this nation.

But that is another story!

3. CYRIL & LAURA WILDING

Cyril

From an early age, I had my childhood snatched from me.

I was twelve years old. A child being sexually abused. Every other week, my cousin would come to the house, asking my mum if he could take me to Bolton swimming baths. This is when the grooming began. Eventually he asked if I could stay for the weekend, and it was at this point that I was introduced to his friends, who also started to sexually abuse me. This happened over a two-year period.

I could not handle the pain I was going through. I was drinking alcohol to numb the pain – cider and vodka – in the run-up to the time my cousin came for me.

I started smoking a bit of weed at the age of thirteen by going to a friend's house. I enjoyed the feeling of getting stoned. Then came the other drugs. First, LSD, then speed, and then the needle when I started to inject speed. Being high on drugs helped me to forget what I was going through. But then came the addiction and that meant I needed money.

I was running around Wigan carrying out robberies, stealing whatever I could to pay for my addiction. I was in and out of the police station every week. I remember one robbery where I was standing outside of one of the banks in Pemberton, Wigan, waiting to find an easy target, and looking for an escape route. This normally involved running through the graveyard before the police caught up with me. I was always scared of being caught.

When I was seventeen I was on the run from the police because of a street robbery in the Wigan area. On another occasion, I got arrested at the scene. The police had been watching me, just waiting to catch me. I didn't have a chance to get away, but managed to get off as the police gave me bail for this crime.

I was consistently getting into gangs and owing dealers money. This led me to relocate to Manchester. I remember once I was on a train with a sawn-off shotgun shoved up my top. After getting off at Victoria train station, I walked up a road with Strangeways prison on my right and Bury New Road on my left. Walking into my sister's house with the gun, she went crazy, shouting at me to get the gun out of her house. Her boyfriend told me of a family that would buy it for £90, but rather bizarrely told me they would also use it, so asked me to clean the gun before I sold it to them!

I remember around this time I was desperate to make a fresh start, but ended up even deeper into drugs, running about with gangsters in Cheetham Hill, selling Class A drugs. I thought I was making a name for myself! I was earning a lot of money, but ended up spending it all on drugs.

It seemed like a natural progression to start buying the drugs in bulk and selling them to friends, and then to their friends. Before I knew it, I was dealing and taking all the profits.

Despite this, I still ended up in debt with people I thought were my friends. Again I needed money, so went back into robbery. At the time I recall stealing a lot of vans on Bury New Road. On one occasion I saw a guy in a van which was full of clothes. I knew I could make good money out of this van, so ended up opening the door and dragging the guy out. Unsurprisingly, he didn't want to give it up, so he got a kicking and I got the van.

The dealers I owed money to got paid, but I had the police on my back again. I was arrested. I also got charged for shoplifting. The police give me bail but told me I had to sign on at the police station every night. The last time I was due to sign on, two police officers were waiting for me and put me on remand for a robbery in the Wigan area.

Finally, my good fortune was over and I was sent to prison for the first time. I had to do six months in Hindley and Stoke Heath prisons. I hated prison. The place stank. On the first day there were guys banging at your door asking for a cigarette and then the bullying started.

When I was released, I got myself into car crime, especially ram raids and smash-and-grabs, because I still needed drugs. I just needed to get off my face. I really enjoyed the feeling drugs gave me – the way drugs going through my body caused me to not feel bothered about anything in life – and yet again I found myself owing the drug dealers money.

Once I remember getting in my car at 2 a.m. and doing a moonlight! I packed my clothes and only took what I knew would fit in my car. I moved to Salford.

I tried to sort my life out, but it didn't work; I just ended up with another prison sentence – but this was going be a long one. I was in a bad car crash, under the influence of drink and drugs. I could have died. I got remanded to Forest Bank prison, where they saw my arms. I had been cutting myself. Not a lot of people knew, but I was a self-harmer. Immediately they put me on a twenty-four hour suicide watch and kept me in the hospital wing, I was in such a bad way. As I had no drugs or drink inside me, all the feelings of being abused as a child came flooding back; the pain was there again. Would it ever stop?

The day after I entered prison, I heard the key at my cell door. An old lady came in.

'Are you OK, son?'

'Do I look OK?'

'I have been told you want to harm yourself,' she said.

Something came with that woman that day. Now I know it was the Holy Spirit.

Picture the scene: this old lady is in my cell on her own, sitting on a chair in front of me, and all I'm doing is crying. She's telling me that all my pain and all my anger, everything I'd been through, Jesus has taken all of it on the cross.

Jesus went through being cut and bruised for me and that meant I didn't need to do it to myself.

It was the first time I was able to tell anyone everything I had been through. I wept many tears as we talked in that cell. I found the love of Jesus. My life started to change from that day on. I even started to help others by becoming a prison listener.

After I came out of prison, I moved to Rochdale, where I started going to church. I loved going to church, but during the week I was still dabbling with drink and drugs. Although I had had a significant experience in that prison cell and knew

Jesus was real, I was still holding on to the pain of the past and felt unable to find help.

At this time I became the manager of a charity shop in Rochdale. One day I got a phone call. It was my sister, telling me that my youngest sister was in intensive care. I immediately got on a train to Wigan hospital, where all my family was waiting.

She died in front of us all.

She had drunk herself to death.

Her body had given up on her due to her alcohol addiction. She was just twenty-nine years old.

I hit the bottle again.

Hard.

I blamed God for my sister's death. I was in a dark place. I was really messed up, drinking and taking drugs. Depression came back and I ended up in my flat cutting my arms again.

I knew I couldn't go on anymore doing things my way.

I had to make a decision.

And I made the best decision that I could ever have made.

I made a phone call to Victory Outreach Christian rehab centre and joined their programme. I was told this was a nine to twelve-month programme, but in my mind I thought I would just do a couple months. As I saw so many ex-addicts talking about freedom in Jesus Christ, I felt I had become part of the family.

Rehab was the making of me! It showed me how to truly have a relationship with Jesus Christ.

It was during my time in rehab that I started to notice Laura in the Bible studies. I will never forget the day I saw her looking to the cross in church and singing. I started to realise she was the one for me. Someone who will look to the cross every day! Now we both serve God at The Message Trust. I am part of The Message Enterprise Centre, carrying out infrastructure building maintenance.

Laura

My parents divorced when I was aged eleven, and it left me with a deep sense of rejection that led me to look for love in all the wrong places.

I craved attention. I realised very quickly that I could get this by acting up in front of my parents, teachers and friends, and especially showing off to boys. I was attracted to the bad boys. I was the one all the mums told their kids to stay away from! I felt I didn't fit in anywhere. I started smoking cannabis, inhaling solvents, and became involved in the rave scene, which led to harder drugs such as amphetamines, pills and acid.

I became depressed and, by the time I was sixteen, I'd tried to commit suicide. I remember being in a relationship with a boy I thought I loved, and he cheated on me. I was devastated and wanted to end my life, so I took an overdose of paracetamol.

I was easily led and fell into one violent relationship after another. Looking back now, I can see I was attracted to men who had drug problems, and because of the way I felt about myself, I thought I didn't deserve anything better.

When I was twenty-one, I was sexually attacked. I ended up in a mental hospital. This was the start of me being in and out of hospital at least twice a year. I lost my job (as a hairdresser), my long-term boyfriend and my home all within a week. Once again I tried to take my life, and became an intravenous heroin and opiate user. I was put on a methadone programme. I was in self-destruct mode and didn't care any more whether I lived or died.

Various stints in rehab never worked, and I was in and out of psychiatric hospitals. It was during this time that I first started to hear about Jesus – about how he could set me free and change me. I was forever meeting Christians!

Then at the age of twenty-four I fell pregnant, but I wasn't mentally or emotionally mature enough to become a mother. I was involved in all sorts of crime and was at the height of my drug addiction. I had my son and kept him for the first eighteen months of his life, but then, after social workers became involved, he went to live with my mum and stepdad. I just couldn't cope.

I first gave my life to God when I was pregnant, and even entered a Christian rehab to try to come off my methadone. I went to church a few times, but deep down I was scared. I carried so much guilt, shame, hurt and pain, and the only thing that took it away was getting wasted.

I ended up homeless again and at the age of twenty-seven I ended up in protective care in a mental institution after being found with a gun, shooting the roof in my new flat, thinking people were after me. I'd lost my mind with drug-induced psychosis. I hadn't slept for about two weeks and had started to hear voices and see things, and thought I was invincible. I had feelings of grandeur and thought people were in awe of me. I had lost the plot. I was so high at one point prior to this, I was swinging off a three-storey building on an iron bar thinking I could fly.

My parents were told I could spend the rest of my life in hospital, but after ten weeks I signed myself out and went straight back into drug addiction. However, this time I was also receiving a high dosage of prescription drugs.

The following two years are a blank to me. I can't remember anything except for the Teen Challenge bus. I'd been to prison for a series of petty crimes, wasn't long out, and was still being tagged. The bus came to my home town every Tuesday and gave out food and drink, and the staff prayed for and encouraged me. I was meeting crazy Christians again! They started to tell me more about Jesus. I liked the sound of this man and really felt drawn to these people; they showed me so much love and care, yet I couldn't understand why they liked me. I felt so unlovable.

Then one night I went along to a service and heard all these different stories from people about how Jesus had set them free from addiction and mental health issues. That night I went forward from my seat to the altar and prayed, 'God, whatever they have, I want it. Please help me.'

After speaking to a few people afterwards, I made the decision to leave that night and go to Manchester to enter the Victory Outreach recovery programme. This was a nine to twelve-month recovery programme, and was the hardest thing I'd ever done in my life. When I arrived I was wearing shorts and a T-shirt and held a phone in my hand. That was all I owned in the world. I spent the next two years in in the rehab home. I was so hurt and broken, but God took hold of my life and started to change me.

Reading the Bible was slowly transforming my mind, and by praying and speaking to God I knew I was drawing closer to him. He was healing my heart as he showed me so much love. He restored the relationship with my family and my son, which was the most important thing for me.

I truly understood that Jesus died for my sins and that he took all my guilt, shame, hurt and pain on that cross, and it no longer belonged to me. How much freedom is that? Better than any drug ever! As I often said at the time, 'There ain't no high but the Most High!'

I felt clean, renewed and restored. I now felt like a woman of dignity, belonging and destiny. I became aware of the Holy Spirit leading my life. I felt safe, secure and loved. For the first time I also had a vision for my future. I graduated from the programme and went to work in The Message Enterprise Centre for The Message Trust, and restarted my career as a hairdresser.

I married Cyril, who I met on the Victory Outreach programme, in September 2014. I've made so many friends – people I can truly trust and rely on – and my life has totally changed. *I've* totally changed!

Now I want help people who are stuck in addiction and mental health issues, and I'm excited for my future and what God has for me. I've been clean for over five years now, and I have done more in these few years than I did in all the years I was addicted.

The Word of God is true; he does restore all the years that have been stolen.

4. CHAZ HOMEWOOD

'Mr Homewood, how do you plead to the charge of armed robbery?'

'Guilty, your Honour,' I said.

'Mr Homewood, you are a prolific, persistent offender and a danger to the community. I hereby sentence you to six years.'

Six years? If I hadn't been handcuffed to the security guards next to me, I would have fallen to the floor. The guards led me out of the court room. I felt like my life was over. I found myself locked in the sweatbox, at the back of an old bus, headed to HMP Lincoln. As the bus bumped along the pothole-littered roads, occasionally throwing my shoulders into the steel walls of the sweatbox, I thought about my life. How did I get here and where did it go wrong?

Growing up, for a time it was just me and Mum. I never knew my dad, only the stories my mum shared with me. To this day, all I know is that he was a Cockney from East London – and a heroin addict. My mum first met him when he was in rehab near Newark. At the time he was doing OK and she fell for his charm and promises. It wasn't long afterwards that she became pregnant with me. But my dad returned to the drugs and was soon injecting all over his body. At one point his feet had become so swollen and infected from injecting that they looked like red balloons.

My mum loved my dad and stayed because she believed that he could quit the drugs. But the final straw came when one day, as a baby, I crawled across the floor and over my dad's swollen feet. My mum says he picked me up and threw me across the room. It was in that moment she decided to go it alone. She took me and left and never looked back.

At the time my mum was only twenty, with not much in the world, and no family to help her. We moved into a very small terraced house that had a shower in my room and an outside toilet in the shed. I hated that toilet. It didn't have a light and in the winter you felt like you were sitting on a block of ice. My mum tried hard to provide what we needed. She held down multiple jobs, but it wasn't enough. So she began to shoplift regularly. I know she did what she had to in order to put food on the table and clothes on my back, and for that I will always be grateful to her. Many times as a young lad I was sat in the back office of a shop feeling nervous, listening to the yelling, and waiting for the police to come and arrest my mother for shoplifting again.

I know now that life was an incredible struggle for my mum, and I can see where it wore her down. She wasn't a drug addict or an alcoholic. She was a strong woman and at one time had big dreams, but nothing had turned out the way she had imagined. Growing up, I can't really remember a time when my mother was affectionate towards me, and most of the time she wasn't around because she was working so much. I spent a large portion of my early childhood alone, waiting for my mother to get off work. Each day after school I had to go to the library or the park and entertain myself until half past seven. That's when my mum finished washing dishes at the local homeless shelter. Some nights I would wake up and find myself alone in the house because my mum was at the local Chinese takeaway, washing dishes. During those years the loneliness was horrible. Even when my mum was home, she was too tired to want to have anything to do with me.

Things changed when I was about seven years old. My mum finally met 'Mr Right'. She had always had boyfriends, but they never seemed to stick around very long – which I was happy about, because they usually weren't nice to me and just seemed to make my mum more unhappy. But when my mum met Dave, things were different. She was finally happy. I remember sitting on the settee and watching them laugh together. I had such an intense feeling of hope for the future; I thought, 'This is finally it.' Dave was nice to me; he used to buy me sweets from the shop and he would take time to talk to me. I began to think we could all be happy together and Dave could be like a dad to me.

For a while, things were good. I started to feel happy and settled. Our little family grew when my mum had my brother, Nils. Of course, Dave and my mum would fight now and again, but generally, they seemed happy.

One day I came home from school and my mum and Dave were standing in the kitchen. As I walked in, they said that they had something to tell me: 'We are all going on holiday to Cornwall.' I was so excited I ran up to my room and started packing. I had never been on a holiday before.

I don't remember much of Cornwall except the swimming pool, as I was in it most of the day. Then, one evening I was walking back to our chalet and as I got closer I could hear shouting. My mum was screaming and pots and pans were smashing into the walls and floor. I opened the door and saw Dave and my mum in front of me, fighting. My mum stopped shouting at Dave and turned to me. She started pointing at me and yelled at Dave, 'Tell him, go on, tell him why you're leaving!'

Dave looked into my eyes and then looked at the floor as he walked straight past me. When he walked out of the door, my mum burst into tears. Eventually she told me that he was leaving her when we got home, but that we were going to try to enjoy the rest of the holiday. I was shattered and so confused. I thought, 'This is crazy.' That same night we went to the holiday entertainment show. We all just sat in silence.

Dave finally got up and went to the bar. My mum turned to me and asked me to take my brother up for the Coolest Kid competition that was going on. I was embarrassed by all of the people, and not in a good mood anyway, so I said, 'No.'

My mum swung around and grabbed my arm hard, squeezing her fingernails into my skin. She put her face close to mine and said, 'It's all your fault. If you'd have been a nice little kid, he wouldn't be leaving. I hate you and I wish you had never been born. You've ruined my life.'

I wrenched my arm away from her and ran off. Later, Dave found me and asked me what had happened. I told him and they began to fight again. Mum screamed at Dave, 'When you leave, take him with you!'

When we returned home, Dave wasted no time in packing his things and leaving. And that was it. He was gone.

My mum couldn't cope and ended up having a breakdown.

Our relationship only got worse. We were both hurt and my brother was too young to know what had happened. When Dave left I was about twelve years old, and this was when things started to go wrong for me. I had always struggled in school with reading and writing, but now I was ten times worse. I couldn't concentrate on anything and my emotions were out of control. In a few seconds I could get so angry that I would destroy things and burst into tears over nothing. I just kept thinking, 'I hate my life. What did I do to deserve this?'

I decided that I would never trust anyone again and never let another person hurt me. The way I looked at the world started to change. I didn't care about pleasing my mum or trying to be good. There were three lads at school who were always getting in trouble and bullied the other kids. I used to avoid them, but now I saw the way that the other kids respected and feared them and I decided I wanted some of that too. So I started hanging out with them. I simply didn't care anymore.

We started out with petty theft, shoplifting smart pens and selling them to the kids at school. I liked my new status and everyone knew me. By the age of thirteen, I was skipping school most days. We moved on from pens to shoplifting bottles of whisky, vodka, brandy, or anything else we fancied. If it was on a shelf, and I wanted it, I took it. We would sell our bottles of alcohol back to local pub owners for £10 per litre, and so began my life of crime. With all the money we were making, we felt like gangsters. We would buy cannabis and get high most days. Soon my friends introduced me to speed and ecstasy, and by the time I was fourteen, I was injecting daily. The drugs helped me to forget the past and the emptiness that seemed to follow me everywhere. They made me feel like a different person. When I was taking them I didn't feel insecure inside, I felt confident. But when the drugs wore off, the sad reality of my life and all the emptiness came rushing back into me.

Still only fourteen, my life was fully out of control. By this time I had become the ringleader of our little criminal rat pack. I stole my first car before I was fifteen. Thieving items off shelves wasn't enough any more; now I was smashing windows to break into shops, and burgling houses all over Newark. I was already classed as a career criminal by the police, who were counting down the days to my fifteenth birthday. They wanted to send me off to a real prison, and not just some youth place.

I turned fifteen in January 1996. By April of the same year, I was in front of a judge, with two of my friends, receiving my first prison sentence, for burglary and selling stolen goods. The judge gave me twelve months at HMP Young Offenders Institution, Onley. At the time of sentencing, I was so spaced out on amphetamines that the entire experience felt like a hallucination.

At Onley, they took me to my cell, and when the door slammed shut it finally dawned on me that this was my new home. My home consisted of a toilet and sink, a table and chair, and a metal bed with a paper-thin mattress.

I spent that first day lying on my bed trying to sort out what was real and what was not. As I glanced out of my small window, I thought I was hallucinating again when I saw what looked like little kites waving in the wind. Later I would find out that this was how we prisoners were able to pass contraband to one another.

To be truthful, prison was an education, but not in the way they had intended. It is true that I was required to attend academic classes in the morning and gym in the afternoon, but that is not where I was gaining my knowledge. It was in the recess and the recreation hall that I got my education. I went into Onley only knowing a few ways to commit crime, but came out only six months later knowing so much more.

Within hours of being released from Onley, I was taking drugs and committing crime. In four months, I was back in prison again. Crime and punishment became my way of life. It got to the point that my life made more sense in prison than outside of it. From the age of fifteen to thirty-one I spent a total of eleven years in prison.

At eighteen, I was introduced to crack cocaine and heroin. From that point on, I became a monster. Now committing violent crimes, I was completely reckless and out of control. I didn't slow down even for a minute to think about what I was doing; everything I did was controlled by a brown or white substance. For the next couple of years, I was in and out of prison.

As I said at the start of my story, at only twenty-one years old, I was headed for HMP Lincoln to serve six years. Now, I started to think about my life. I had been told this lifestyle was about Ferraris, mansions, and getting with hot women, but in reality my life has been nothing but suffering and pain. I didn't want to be an addict and I didn't want to be locked up for the next six years. My partner at the time was pregnant and I hated the thought that my son would have to grow up without me, just like I had had to grow up without my dad. So I decided in that moment that I wanted to change my life.

I put everything I had into it. I requested a drug-free wing, had weekly drug tests, and went on a rehab programme. I also completed the Enhanced Thinking Skills programme, which is designed to help you weigh up the pros and cons of your decisions, and took a Victim Awareness course, so that I would understand the effects of my actions on others. I used every resource the Government said that someone like me needed in order to change.

After three years, my parole hearing came up, but I was knocked back because of my previous offences. I was gutted, but because they'd seen a change in me they were going to give me a chance. I was going to be recommended for an open prison. I thought, 'Great! Here's my chance to sort my life out.' I was charged up on good intentions and ready for a little freedom.

Sadly, after arriving at the open prison, the new-found freedom brought back old temptations and gave me easy access to drugs. I had tried so hard to change and I had failed. Within weeks I was hooked on heroine and smoking cannabis.

One night I sat on my bed and said to myself, '*Why?!* Why am I like this, and why can't I change?'

A little voice within me said, 'This is all you are and this is all you'll ever be.'

And with that I jumped up off the bed, and ran out across the field to a house nearby. I broke into the shed and used a screwdriver to steal their car. I had it in my mind to do one last robbery and to hell with everything else, but then an image of my son flashed across my mind. He had been born while I was in prison and I had never got to see him.

I headed for Newark. It was late by the time I arrived. I knocked and my son's mother opened the door. She was about five foot two with long brown curly hair, brown eyes, and smooth skin. We had a long history. We had been partners on and off since I was sixteen. But after my son was born she didn't visit any more; she had moved on with her life.

As soon as she laid eyes on me she began to yell, 'What have you done? You're so stupid! How could you do this?'

Eventually she calmed down and let me inside the house. She made me something to eat and we started to talk. She paused and said, 'I've got something to tell you, Chaz.'

I said, 'OK, let's hear it.'

'I've become a born again Christian,' she said, looking serious. I nearly fell off the back of my chair, I was so surprised. I started to laugh, but she was still serious.

I began to mock her. 'Are you telling me you really believe that stuff? If there is a God, then why is the world so messed up? Why is there so much pain and suffering?'

She shook her head. 'I don't know, Chaz. I don't have all the answers, but I heard something in church today. It's a story in the Bible about the wise and the foolish builders. Right now you are being the foolish builder, who built his house – your life – on sand. You've built your life on drugs, crime, money and sex. And they will only bring your life crashing down, until it is nothing, just like it is now. But the wise builder is the person who builds their house on the rock, which is Jesus.'

I didn't really understand what she was saying, but her

words cut through me and left a burning sensation in my heart. I was silent and she continued, 'Chaz, God loves you and he knows what you've been through, He knows how much you are hurting inside, and how much you want to be loved. If you ask Jesus into your life, he will make you a new person. He can give you the strength to do the things you can't do on your own.' I didn't want to hear what she was saying, but I couldn't shake her words off.

She got up from the table and said, 'I'm going to bed now. I'll leave you to think about all of this.' Walking into her bedroom, she shut the door behind her and I was alone. I finished my meal and settled on the settee. Those words, the sand, the rock, Jesus is the rock, kept rolling around in my mind. There was something different about them. I couldn't sleep for most of the night; I wrestled with thoughts of God. I started to think, 'What if he is real and he does love me? And what if he can help me change my life?' Up to now I knew I had made a total mess of it. At some point I drifted off to sleep, but before I did I had already decided what I was going to do.

I woke up in the morning to the sound of breakfast being prepared. My son's mum was in the kitchen. I went into my son's room and spent some time with him. After a while, his mum came and stood at the door to the room. I looked up and told her to phone the police. I wanted to hand myself in. The look on her face was surprised and then relieved. She made the call and within five minutes the police were at the door. I was headed back to HMP Lincoln.

When I got there I put my name down for chapel. I had been to chapel many times before, but it was just a cover to score drugs. This time it was different. As I walked up the steps of the chapel, a thick wave of emotion hit me and I began to cry, something I hadn't done for many years. I started to feel bad for all the things I had done. Halfway up the chapel aisle I was sobbing violently and freaking out because I couldn't control it. I wiped my face on my sleeves and I could see my old friends sitting there, watching me.

I kept walking towards the front of the chapel, and sat down. A man I had never seen before stood up and said, 'God gave me a message for someone in here today. He told me to tell you that he knows where you are in life right now, and he knows the suffering and pain that you've been through. If you will turn and pray to him, he will heal you.'

Just like the night before, the words pierced me and I knew the message was for me. I continued to cry throughout the chapel service. I could feel something shifting in my heart.

At the end of the service the man walked over to me and said, 'Do you want all of your suffering and pain to end?'

I said, 'Yes.'

We prayed together and I surrendered my life to Jesus. I wanted to build my life on the rock. I didn't see any flashing lights or hear a big bang, but I knew something had happened inside me. I will never forget that day, it was 4 September 2005. Over the next months, I read my Bible as much as I could, even though some of it was hard to understand. I started going to all of the Bible studies and chapel services and began to experience the presence of God. I now knew that he loved me.

I wish that I could tell you that my life was plain sailing from this point on, that I was instantly changed and never did drugs or crime again, but that would be a lie. I've heard of people being instantly delivered and I know it happens. But that is not what happened with me. In the end it took two rehabs, another four-year prison sentence and nearly dying for me to realise it has to be God's way, not mine.

The real turning point in my life came in 2011. I was back in prison again after only being out for three short weeks. I was devastated. I thought, 'I can't do this anymore. I'm a hypocrite. I want to be a man of God, but I can't. I'm going to end it all.' So I tried to kill myself in my prison cell. It was by the grace of God that someone found me when they did, or I wouldn't be here to tell this story.

After the incident, I was put on suicide watch for a couple of days and then returned to a normal cell. Again, I fell into old habits. I swapped tobacco for some Subutex and sniffed it in my cell, but it didn't make me feel any better. For a long time, drugs hadn't had the same effect on me as they used to, because now I would just start thinking about God and what it felt like to be in his presence. I loved God and missed him. I knew I was running from him again and it made me sad.

I started to pray out loud in my cell and I didn't care who could hear me. Kneeling on the floor I cried and said to God, 'I'm so sorry, God, please help me. Please take this from me, I keep going back to it. Heal me, God, please. I don't want this.' I prayed for a while and then I felt God's presence fill my prison cell. Then God spoke so clearly to me. The voice wasn't audible, it was as though he spoke the words straight into my heart. He told me that my life of drug addiction and crime was finished and that he was going to intervene; that this would all just be a thing of the past. He told me that he was going to heal me and restore me. He said that a time was coming when I would be strong and passionate for the things of God and that he would use me for his glory. He also spoke specific things about the wife that he was bringing me and that I would have a family. For a long time I just laid on my bed and enjoyed the feelings of peace and joy. I thought about the words God spoke, and at some point I drifted off to sleep.

In the morning I woke up and started to read my Bible. As I was reading from the book of Genesis, a verse just seemed to jump out at me. In the passage – chapter 12 verse 1 – God was speaking to Abraham, saying, 'Leave your … father's house, and go to the land that I will show you' (NLV). It's hard to explain but I knew what God was telling me to do. I needed to leave Newark. It was a very difficult decision to make because my son was there, and I loved seeing him. I had to trust that if God wanted me to do it, then it was for the best. I carried on trusting God with a new sense of his hand on my life. Two weeks later, a prison chaplain came to my cell. He said, 'Chaz, if you are ready to change your life, there is a room for you at a place called the Lighthouse.'

I jumped off my bed and said, 'I'm ready!' I knew this was God working. Two months later I arrived at the Lighthouse with nothing but the clothes on my back.

That was over four years ago. I can say that God has fulfilled every word he spoke to me when I cried out to him on that night. Every day I thank him for the miracles I have seen him do in my life and in other people's. By God's grace and faithfulness I have been completely drug-free. I am now a senior support worker at the Lighthouse Homes Project, based in Rotherham. It is the first job I have ever had. I also have a great relationship with my son. I see him every month. I visit with my mum regularly and God has restored our relationship.

About three years ago I met the beautiful woman who is now my wife. She is American and we met while she was still living in the United States. We have seen God do miracle after miracle in our relationship and in the visa process for her move to the UK. God has blessed our marriage and we are expecting our first child.

I am humbled to say that God has used me for his glory. He has taken me on mission trips to Romania and Macedonia. He has used me in sharing my testimony in schools and churches in the local area, as well as preaching at my church. I am blessed that he uses me every day as I work at the Lighthouse and reach out to guys who have come from the same place that I have been. He has opened doors of opportunity I would never have been able to imagine for myself. He is truly a good Father who loves and looks after his children. He is faithful, even if the journey is a long one. He never leaves you or gives up on you. I had to learn to trust him and he did the rest.

5. BRIAN PORTER

I was six years old when my life began to unravel.

I lived with my mum, dad, older half-brother and sister from my mum's previous marriage, and three younger sisters in a modest house in Penwortham near Preston.

I was blissfully unaware that my dad was a sick pervert who was addicted to sleeping tablets, and enjoyed bringing strange men home to force my mum to have sex with while he watched. He was also abusing my siblings on a regular basis. My best friend and closest companion was Ben, my dog; he went everywhere with me and would always listen to me as I told him my secrets, dreams and problems.

Then one day I returned home from primary school to find several fire engines blocking the street. One of the fire fighters came up to me and told me that our house had been burned down. I later learned that my mum had suffered a mental breakdown and had gone round each room setting fires. Ben had been asleep and had been killed by the smoke. My mum was arrested for arson and sent to prison for three months.

We were moved to an empty house with my dad in a village near Chorley. We had no possessions and had to get hand-outs from the local church. In the space of one day I had lost my mum, my best friend, Ben, my school friends, my clothes, my toys – in fact, my entire identity.

I started at the local primary school and did not easily make new friends. The kids had learned of the fire, my mum's incarceration and the fact that we were wearing church cast-offs, and kids can be cruel. They would taunt me constantly, calling me a tramp or my mother a jailbird. I became very angry with the other kids and the world in general.

I began hitting back at all of it. I would throw chairs across the classroom and spent a lot of time in the head teacher's office being told that I was a bad boy who would never amount to anything.

The last time I visited the head's office was at the hands of a dinner lady who had got on my wrong side on the wrong day. I asked her if she could only give me a few beans as I did not like them. She made a nasty comment about how I should be happy to eat anything I was offered, as beggars couldn't be choosers. The other kids began to laugh and I lost my temper. She dragged me through the dining hall and up the open-plan staircase to the head's office, but I elbowed her in the stomach, causing her to lose her balance and fall over the bannister onto the tiled floor beneath, fracturing her skull and breaking her collarbone.

The head screamed at me that I was out of the school and I was pure evil.

'At last,' I thought. 'I have an identity.'

I was expelled, and sent to a day reform school for troubled boys in Chorley.

I found that this environment was challenging as all the boys there were from broken homes, and as a result were trying to make their mark by being tough and pushing back against the world that had rejected them. As a result I had to step up my game. I found new ways of expressing myself through the medium of aggression and violence. My time there was cut short when another boy and I picked up the English teacher's chair, and tipped him backwards out of the first-floor window, breaking his neck and subsequently putting him in a wheelchair for the rest of his life. I was expelled from that school. They thought I was evil too.

My inner rage had a good reason for growing and darkening. My mum had been released from prison and my dad had just gone – no warning or build-up; he was just there one day and gone the next. I had no idea why. At that time I was not aware that my dad was a sexual predator and a paedophile. I just became angrier at everything and everyone.

Then I was sent away to a boarding school in Rochdale, which was a hotbed of abuse. So I spent the next six years fighting every single day either to prove myself or to prevent a sexual attack from both the staff and older boys.

At the age of fourteen I was assessed by a psychologist and he diagnosed me as high-functioning autistic. As a result of this diagnosis, the powers-that-be began holding meetings about me and determined that I was worthy of attending a boarding school in Yorkshire for gifted boys. These were probably the best three years of my teenage life, as all the other boys came from a similar background to me, and although we fought in the usual adolescent manner, we never did so out of hatred or a desire to truly hurt one another. Besides, I was so good at fighting that I was seldom fearful of losing.

I left there at the age of seventeen and immediately joined

the Army. I spent eighteen months in the Royal Engineers. This came to an end when I realised that I had spent years of my life sharing a dormitory with other males and had had enough of living in an institution. I left and became a wine waiter in a large hotel. This was near the house I now lived in with my mum and stepdad, as well as the couple of siblings who were left at home and not in care of some sort.

I met a girl and, for the first time in my life, I felt I mattered to another person on an emotional level. We married just after my nineteenth birthday and spent three years living in a flat. We enjoyed taking drugs and would smoke weed and take acid and speed together at the weekends.

Then, when I was twenty-one, my wife became pregnant. I was so happy, and decided that this would be the making of me. However, things didn't turn out as I expected. While my wife had stopped taking drugs the instant she found out she was carrying a child, I had no such incentive and continued to take drugs throughout her pregnancy. On the night she went into labour I had taken a large amount of speed and was completely out of it for the full twenty-two hours until my son was born. And when he came home I found myself resenting him. He took my wife's time and attention away from me and I became jealous of my baby.

I went in search of another outlet for my need to belong to something, and on that search I came across heroin. Heroin was exactly what I had been looking for, as it not only numbed the pain of my past but stopped me feeling any emotion at all. I thought it freed me, but the reality was it chained me up tightly.

So began sixteen years of my life that would take me so far from myself and my three children that it would need a miracle to ever make it back.

After my first year in the chains of addiction, I was back at home and desperately trying to stay clean when I was invited to hear Barry Woodward speak at a small church in Leyland. I found that he was speaking right into my life, and after the service someone bought me a copy of his book, *Once an Addict*. I asked him to sign it for me. He did so, and he also wrote a reference to Scripture that he said God had given him for me. It was Jeremiah 29:11: "'For I know the plans I have for you,' declares the LORD, "plans to prosper you and not to harm you, plans to give you hope and a future'" (NIV, 2011). I was led through what they called 'the sinner's prayer', where I said sorry for everything I had ever said or done wrong to hurt God and other people, and I accepted Jesus as the boss of my life, believing he had died on the cross to take the punishment for all my wrongdoing, to make me right with God. Soon afterwards I was baptised at that church.

Life went well for about eight months and then I foolishly thought that I no longer needed to go to church. It took just six months for me to fall back into my negative patterns of behaviour and I went back to my addiction, worse than ever.

The word 'gangster' is thrown about all too easily these days and young people link it to some kind of appealing and powerful way of being, but the truth is far more disturbing.

I began working for a very scary man as a way of feeding my own habit, and I was quickly noticed as an asset to his firm. I was promoted through the ranks until in just two years we were actually partners and were running three-quarters of Preston's underbelly.

I was committing violent crimes and selling large amounts of misery to other addicts.

I would think nothing of putting my gun into the mouth of someone who owed us money and causing them to really fear for their lives. I thrived on the fear and was drunk with power. People feared me, which I mistook for respect and kidded myself that I had found my identity and true calling. But this line of work comes with occupational hazards, such as prison or retaliation, and I experienced both several times. I was shot twice, stabbed twice, and spent some time in various prisons.

Eventually, my addiction took over completely and I began to get sloppy. I was spending more on drugs then I was earning from selling the stuff, and I was not eating or sleeping, which meant that I was not on form and could not fight the way I used to.

As a result of this, rival gangsters were able to catch me off guard and began to get the better of me by taking advantage of my weakened state. I ended up fearing for my life and went on the run, spending time in a desolate squat in a high-rise block of flats in Preston.

Within six months my health was so bad that I was unable to stand up or even go to the toilet. I was four and a half stone, I could barely breathe and was in constant pain. Eventually, I was forced to get into an ambulance by the police, who said it was either hospital or the police station as it was for my own good. The hospital diagnosed me with advanced pneumonia and told me that I had very little chance of lasting more than three days. They put tubes in my stomach to feed me, which I pulled out. I told them to just leave me to die as I deserved nothing more.

Two days later I was quite literally at death's door when my wife brought my children in to see me. She told me that I had to get well to give my kids the opportunity to know me, and that to just die would be a selfish and cowardly thing for me to do. I pulled myself up in the bed and asked a nurse to bring me some porridge, which she immediately did. For the next eight weeks I just ate anything and everything that was available. I also had a tube stuck into my back to drain the rotten mucus from my chest cavity which had caused my left lung to explode.

About halfway through my twelve-week stay in the hospital I was on my way to the bathroom when a little old Italian lady approached me and told me that I had friends in high places. I immediately thought she was talking about the gangsters I had run with, but she went on to say that someone 'up there' was watching out for me, and that everything would be OK. I thanked her politely and carried on, even though in my head I was thinking, 'Crazy old bat!' The next morning I heard that the lady had died in the night and I began to feel guilty for thinking badly of her.

When her family arrived to see her I approached a man who I now know to be her son and I offered my condolences to him. I then went on to tell him that I had only been speaking to her the evening before, and that she had told me that I would be OK and that someone 'up there' was watching out for me. He just stared at me for a moment, and then went on to tell me that my claim was not possible as his mother could not speak a word of English. Needless to say, this threw me, and I went away questioning everything.

About a year later, me and two friends bought some heroin, but when we cooked it up we noticed it had an orange colour to it and did not look right, but we were withdrawing and so we took that risk. There was Anthrax in that batch of heroin and as a result I lost my left hip through a serious infection that had me in hospital for seven months fighting to keep my leg. My friends were not so fortunate. The first one died twelve minutes after injecting it into his arm and the second was dead on arrival at the hospital. Once again I had been spared, but why? Was it because from the moment I had given my life to God he had held me in his everlasting arms and was keeping me safe, even in my bad choices and my ignorance to his love and his will for my life?

When I came out of hospital I immediately began using heroin again, and as I had nowhere to live, I found myself on the streets begging for change to feed my addiction. I had developed large open abscesses on my legs and was becoming increasingly unwell.

I was sleeping behind a skip, from which I also ate scraps of food. I had no self-worth and no reason to carry on living. I hadn't seen my children for a long time and their mother had made it clear that she did not want anything more to do with me. She had divorced me while I was using drugs and I had signed the papers from my hospital bed as I did not want to cause her any more pain.

One night, sitting in a shop doorway with a friend of mine

sitting on the opposite side of the street, both of us begging for change, a group of lads on their way home from the clubs stopped and began talking to my friend. I thought that they may be about to give him something. But they started to kick and punch him. Then one of the lads produced a tin of lighter fluid and squirted it all over my friend in his sleeping bag. They lit a match and set him on fire, then they watched until he was completely aflame, before running off laughing. He screamed in agony as his sleeping bag melted onto his skin, and as he burned to death I just sat hiding in fear, crying, and feeling helpless.

It was not long after this that I decided I had had enough and it was time for me to end it all. I bought six bags of heroin and forty Valium tablets. I was going to overdose. I sat there in the rain, begging, with thoughts of my children spinning in my head. People passed by and either swore at me, spat at me, kicked me, or just told me I was worthless. I felt that the world was confirming that it had no use for me, and that I would be doing the right thing by killing myself.

But just as I turned to pick up my blanket and leave to go and take my own life, a Street Pastor knelt down beside me, put her hand on my shoulder and said these words: 'God has called you to much better than this.' Immediately all thoughts of suicide left me and I began to wonder if God was really up there. More importantly, did he still care for me?

That night I went behind my skip and with tears streaming down my face, I cried out to God.

I asked him to forgive me and said that I wanted to change but had gone too far. I just asked him if I could get to see my children and tell them I was sorry and I loved them, before I died; that would be enough.

When I awoke early the next morning I had an idea in my mind that I knew must have been from God, because it was ridiculous. I felt that I was to just turn up on Christmas Eve at my ex-wife's house and knock on the door. I quickly dismissed this notion as I knew that her reaction would not be welcoming, and I did not want to cause any more upset to my kids.

However, the idea would not go away.

So on the morning of Christmas Eve 2010, I set off. I knocked on the door and it was opened by my eldest son who gave me a hug and let me in. His mum and the two younger children were out so he made me a cup of tea and we talked for a while about school and his expectations for Christmas.

After about an hour, the door opened and in walked my ex-wife and my other kids. They ran up to me and embraced me, but my ex-wife just stood there in disbelief.

'Can Daddy stay for Christmas?' my youngest asked, eagerly. She was not about to break their hearts and so she replied, 'I guess so.'

We had a good Christmas together, and as soon as I could, I got myself on a methadone prescription. I began visiting them as often as I could and even though I was still sleeping rough I managed to stick to my methadone and away from street drugs.

After a couple of months my ex offered me her couch to sleep on, as she said that she could see that I was trying and she didn't want me to go back to my old ways. Things were OK and I got to see my kids, but something was missing. I had stopped taking heroin but had found nothing to fill the hole that it left.

During the time that I had been on the streets, my son had seen a leaflet for CAP (Christians Against Poverty) and given it to his mum as he was sick of her complaining that she did not have enough money. As a result of this, she had received support and practical help from a local community church.

One day my ex-wife said to me, 'Why don't you offer to do some volunteering with the church?' She knew I had previously been to church and thought it might be a good way of occupying my time.

I began helping out in the Inside Out ministry which decorated, cleaned and delivered furniture to people on a low income. I started to attend the services on a Sunday morning and was made very welcome. I helped out in the car parking team and served coffee between the two services. I attended that church for almost two years and was really connecting with good people, but I still had my dependency to methadone and was even actually using heroin on occasion.

Then one Sunday morning during the service the preacher quoted a scripture from the book of Revelation that says 'But since you are like lukewarm water, neither hot nor cold, I will spit you out of my mouth' (3:16, NLT).

I immediately felt that God was speaking to me and convicting me of the fact that I was living a lie, a double life, and I needed to give myself completely to one or the other. I knew that I would have to go into detox and then rehab and process my emotions instead of running and hiding from them as I had done for so long, but the thought of doing so scared me immensely. I prayed to God for guidance and he told me not to worry as he would be there with me all the way and I could rest on him when things became too much for me.

With that assurance I made the arrangements and attended detox and then went into rehab at Littledale Hall near Lancaster.

I decided that I would attend the local Methodist church during my time there and keep my relationship with God at the core of my treatment programme.

The first day I walked into the doors of Brookhouse Methodist Church I noticed a plaque on the wall in the foyer. It was Jeremiah 29:11. I looked up and said out loud, 'OK, I get it, I surrender all I have to your will for my life!'

I have now been at Brookhouse since January 2013. I ran a café there for two years, I help run a youth club at a sister church in Morecambe and am a trustee of that church. We have a food bank and we are trying to reach out to the local community. I am married to Sarah, one of the leaders from the church, and life is good.

Just as I was getting ready to leave rehab, I was examined by a physiotherapist for severe back pain and she told me that my bottom two vertebrae had begun to crumble and my quad muscle in my left knee had completely wasted away. The prognosis was that within a matter of months I would be confined to a wheelchair for the rest of my life. The future seemed bleak and I blamed God for allowing this to happen to me.

The following Sunday I attended the church, not knowing that the night before Sarah had heard from God. He was telling her to pray for me for healing. I had absolutely no intention of going forward for prayer, but someone asked me to take her forward as she was nervous and so I walked her to the front.

Sarah approached me and said that she wanted to pray for me, to which I replied arrogantly, 'No thanks! I don't need it today.' But she persisted and I relented. She prayed to God for healing for me, and I prayed with her.

About an hour after I returned to the supported housing where I was living at the time, I noticed that something was different but I could not figure out what. I knew that something had changed. Then I realised that the pain that I had felt with every single step that I had taken for thirteen years had gone! I jumped up and down and ran up and down the stairs, but nothing could make my hip or my back hurt. This was strange. I made an appointment to see the physiotherapist as soon as possible and two weeks later I went to have the same tests done. When she came into the room with the results, I could see she was struggling to comprehend what was going on.

'I do not understand this, but your back is completely fine, no crumbling of the spine to be seen, and it has even straightened up. Also, your quad muscle seems to be fully restored and your thigh bone is now somehow not clicking against your pelvis as it has done. What happened?'

I told her that I had simply been prayed for.

Following a brief testimony that I shared at the church the week before I completed treatment at rehab, I was approached by a few of my friends at the church who said they thought I should think about preaching, but I dismissed the idea as I already had plans for the things I wanted to do now I had my life back. It was a few months later when the Lord himself put the idea to me, and when he did he left no room for dismissal. He reminded me that I had surrendered my life to him and that his plans for my life were infinitely better than my own had proved to be.

So now I am busier than I have ever been and I have a real sense of purpose and self-worth because I can now see myself through God's eyes – and if he loves me in the way he does and finds me worthy of his time, then who am I to argue with the Lord of creation?

I am slowly letting go of the need to know everything about the future and be in control of all possible outcomes, and simply trusting that whatever tomorrow may bring, my heavenly Father is already there straightening the paths for me.

Believing in God was, I suppose, the easy part for me. I knew he had to exist because I knew that the devil did, as I had worked for him for a long time. Accepting that God believed in me was the thing that I struggled to get my head round. I now work for him, and the devil does not like that one bit. But whenever the enemy tries to throw me off course and remind me of my sinful past, I just turn to God and am reminded of all that he has brought me through. No matter how far I was running in the opposite direction, and how far I felt I had gone away from God, the moment I turned around and cried out to him, he was right there.

God has a plan for each and every one of us, and that plan is to prosper us and not to harm us, to give us a hope and a future! But in order to get all that God has for us, we need to give him all that we are – not just some, but every part of our lives should be lived in full surrender to his will for us.

If you are following Jesus, there is a cost. Sometimes it's difficult, and you feel like you are up against the world. But I've found that when you put everything into God's hands, you begin to see God's hands in everything. This world would have you believe that it is not cool to follow Jesus. But going along with the world for an easy life gives you anything but an easy life – because you are, in effect, going against God. I pray that you will open your heart to what God wants to bless you with, and that your eyes will be opened to his amazing love and power, which reminds me that 'In all these things I am more than a conqueror through him who loved me' (see Romans 8:37).

May the Lord bless you!

6. JOHN WILSON

As I walked down the hallway to my mum's room, I just knew deep down something was wrong – her light was on.

I pushed the door open. She was surrounded by an empty bottle and pills. I stood over her in the silence. I was eight years old.

Up until that point in my childhood, everything seemed normal. I had two younger brothers, and I felt safe and secure, even though my father was not living with my mother any more. But that night, everything changed. I went from feeling secure to feeling rejected, feeling loved to feeling unloved, and feeling safe to feeling very scared. Everything in my world had changed in a single moment.

In the semi-darkness of the room I started to panic. I thought my mum was dead. Then she started to mumble. She wasn't making any sense. I managed to get one of my brothers out of bed and we ran as fast as we could down the street to the phone box. We found my father's new number in the phone book, but he didn't answer, thinking it was a hoax call.

For years we watched our mum fighting her demons. We had frequent visits from social workers, which I hated, and had to stay with different family members. Many mornings we would get up to find strange people in our house after Mum's late-night parties, often with a window broken or another part of our home wrecked.

The time came when my mum and the three of us moved into our grandparents' house so that they could try to help to get some sort of order and normality back into our family. I remember all four of us being cramped up in the spare room. I grew up as a very angry little boy with a lot of hate in my heart, and would often lash out.

My mum tried her best to provide for us, but her job was working in a bar, not the best place for an alcoholic . . .

My dad was a hard grafter and would usually see us on a Saturday, but wasn't really there for us.

As I got older, things began change. Mum started to be a lot better and the family seemed to be getting sorted out. The family finally settled into a new home. My brothers and I went to a new school and all seemed to be going well. However, I was a lost and broken boy carrying many hurts and pains, and this started to affect my schoolwork and relationships. I found it hard to concentrate, often becoming the class clown. I was playing up at home, too, fighting with my brothers and my mum.

Many times social services tried to put me into a home, but my auntie or my dad stepped in and would allow me to live with them for a short while. I developed a mind-set that no one really cared. If my mother had cared for us, I thought, she wouldn't have tried to take her own life. I was often told, 'You will amount to nothing!' Family members would blame me for my mum being ill, and I would blame my mum for the way I was turning out. This was the way it was for years, growing up as a child and into adulthood.

In my time of desperation, loneliness and hurt, always finding it hard to fit in with the right crowd, I began to drink; I was twelve years old. It was the normal thing to do at weekends – down by the beach, everyone getting drunk, falling out and having the odd fight. But a sneaky weekend drink became the odd midweek bottle. I felt a part of something, I was accepted, people liked me.

Like most kids growing up, I had dreams, and my dream was to join the British Army, play the drums in the pipe band and travel the world. I was already in the Army Cadets and played with the local pipe band. I wasn't very good at school, so I put a lot of time and effort into playing the drums. I was good at it; we played at competition level, I was taught by a world champion, and again I found acceptance.

By the time I was old enough to apply to join the Army, my weekend drinking with the 'crew' had moved onto other things. I had started smoking dope at the age of twelve and dabbling with other drugs. I wouldn't say I was hooked on hard drugs back then, but dope was an everyday part of my life. I was just doing what the 'crew' was doing – having a bit of fun, camping out, getting high, being antisocial at times, but it wasn't an issue. Then, when I applied to join the Army, I faced rejection once again as I was refused entry, having failed a medical. It was at this point that I hit the self-destruct button. I lost all hope, was low in self-confidence, and had no plan-B for my life.

I realised that I had to look at a different route for my life. I attended college, which I hated, and left. At this time, I was living with my father and he made it clear that if I was staying in his house I needed to be working. I found no problem in getting a job. As I started working, the money started coming in. This was a good thing, as my drug dependency was growing. My smoking cannabis all day every day soon got interrupted by hard drugs. I would take 'party drugs' at the weekend, but as they sneaked into my midweek life, the weekend party soon became an everyday party. I was no longer in control of when I took the drugs; instead, they began to control me. I needed them to function.

I began to steal and do a bit of dealing to fund my habit. As I got deeper and deeper into the life of an addict, I was soon kicked out of the family home, once again feeling rejected and lonely. My life was spiralling out of control. I had started to commit crimes. I upset people; I'd rip them off, and I was dodging paying my dealers the money owed to them for my supply.

I moved from my home town, Prestonpans, to the city of Edinburgh. It was here that I experienced homelessness for the first time. I had no job, no family, no friends. I had given up the only good thing I was good at, drumming in the pipe band, in exchange for becoming good at taking drugs.

My first night in a hostel, I sat on my bed, thinking, 'Where did it all go wrong?' I looked back over my childhood and that night when I'd found my mum had overdosed. I remembered the many times she'd tried to take her own life, or had ended up ill in hospital because of the drink. And then I suddenly realised what it was like to be an addict; how it felt, how I knew my life was heading in the wrong direction, but I didn't know how to fix it.

It didn't take me long to be introduced to heroin. When I smoked it for the first time, I felt all my problems disappear. I soon found that if I injected the heroin I would get more stoned, and of course that's what I did. I didn't want to feel the pain of my problems anymore.

Heroin had become my new best friend and my demon all in one. It wasn't long before all the other drugs were discarded as I got hooked on heroin. My mate and I would set off every day on the lookout for our next hit. We would go robbing together, we would score together, and we would finish up sleeping on the streets together. We were kicked out of every hostel in Edinburgh for one thing or another. We would find ourselves sleeping in car parks, or in bushes in Princes Street Gardens.

I remember one morning being woken up by men from the council who were throwing sticks at us to see if we were dead. Life on the streets became part of who I was. It was hard work, trying to feed our habit and find a safe place to stay, until we stumbled across an old building, where we were able to kick the door in and make it our home – a squat. It was warm and cosy, all lit up with candles we would steal out of the local church on a daily basis, and we had sleeping bags we'd received from the soup van.

I didn't have time to think about life or normality as the heroin gripped me. I was 'out of it' every day and didn't really understand about the withdrawals until one cold morning when I woke up and discovered my mate had done a runner with the gear. I'd thought that we were partners in crime – brothers looking out for each other – but when you're a drug addict, you care for no one apart from yourself. I should have known that.

That day was tough. I was sweating, hot one minute, cold the next. I was weak, I could hardly walk, but I knew I had to go and get a fix somehow. I would have done anything for that hit of gear – I'd have sold my granny.

I lived on the streets for months. I was stinking, lost loads of weight, was down to nine stone; I was eating out of bins at the back of the supermarket. I knew I had to change but I didn't know how. I would turn up at my mum's house hoping she would take me in.

'No!' was her response. 'I've given you more than enough chances, but you won't stop taking drugs.'

I remember turning up one time after I had been stabbed in the back of the leg, hoping she would give me just one more chance. I promised her I would stop taking drugs.

'No,' she said. 'Phone your dad.'

So I did. This was something I hadn't done before. I always thought he didn't care. He came to my mum's place and for the first time in my life I actually saw a caring side to him.

He turned to my mum. 'Look at him. He's dying! I think he's learned his lesson.'

'No!' Mum replied. 'If you're that concerned, let him stay with you.'

I remember that drive to my dad's house. I felt a bit relieved that I didn't need to sleep another night on the streets. My dad said, 'I'm willing to let you live with us, but I don't know if your brothers will allow you to. If they don't, you can stay the rest of the week and I'll help you get a place.'

My two brothers had every right not to allow me back in the house. When my dad had asked me to leave a year or so before, they were laughing at me as I walked out of the door with my bag of belongings. I'd said to myself, 'They won't be laughing when they come back from work tomorrow.' I'd broken into the house the next day and robbed them. The police were actually still looking for me.

My brothers said I could move back in, but one wrong move and I was out.

'You have one month to get a job and start paying your way,' said Dad. 'And you need to pay your brothers back for what you stole from them.'

I got off the gear, got a job and started doing what I used to do, smoke dope on a daily basis and party hard at the weekends. But it all went quickly wrong and I soon found myself asked to leave the family home, losing yet another job, facing rejection again – all my own fault.

I decided to relocate to a small town called Arbroath. Things were great to begin with. For a start, the police didn't know me. I lived with a friend until I got my own place. He gave me a job on his window-cleaning round and I was hiding my drug use pretty well. Then I met a girl, and we moved in together.

But it wasn't long before I lost my job and found myself hooked back on heroin, and amphetamines. I started to commit crime again, was arrested and locked up. And then I was handed a custodial sentence.

I settled into prison life easily. If I'm honest, it was a nice break from the world. I got clean for a few months, and had no intention of going back on the gear . . . until I got out, and called a dealer.

I remember waiting on a big backdated giro. It was a Saturday morning and I was woken up with a loud bang. I knew it wasn't the postman! It was the police, giving me an early morning wake-up call. I had been getting revenge on my old boss for sacking me. I had spent months on his window-cleaning round, collecting all his money – without him knowing. I was getting away with it so I started collecting all the other window cleaners' money too, and now the police were kicking in my door to arrest me.

I was withdrawing badly, and there was no way for me to get out; we lived in a flat and I didn't fancy the jump.

I was questioned by the police later in the day, then charged. I knew I wouldn't be getting bail and there was no chance of any community order. I couldn't help but think of my girl sat there with my giro, getting high.

However, for some reason they did release me on bail. I was home, my giro was still there – my girl hadn't cashed it in! It was time to get smashed. But that week would be the end of our three-year relationship. Some of the people I'd upset had caught up with me, and my girlfriend had gone to her mum for help. And now she had had enough. So I was sat in my flat all alone, feeling lonely and rejected once again, and all I had was my friend heroin and a burst lip.

The following morning I woke up wondering how I could make a quick score, then I remembered a few customers from the window-cleaning round. Off I went to the first house.

'Window cleaner!' I said.

The lady replied, 'I'll just get you the money.'

She disappeared, then came back and handed me the cash. But as I turned and walked out of the gate, I saw the police driving past. I started to run but the next minute I was on the ground, with the copper saying, 'I've got you now! You're going down.'

As I sat in the cell waiting for the judge to call me up the following morning, I was a bit relieved knowing I was going back to jail. I had lost my girlfriend, my family didn't care, and I had received a bit of a kicking a few days before, so the sound of a holiday at Her Majesty's pleasure sounded OK right then.

I stood in front of the judge, confirmed my name, and gave my plea.

'Guilty,' I said.

He gave me the speech they usually do before giving me the time I was to serve. Then he said, 'Mr Wilson, upon your release from prison, this time I suggest that you go to the Havilah project which is run by Jim and Tracey McLeod at St Andrew's church. You will get the help you need to come off drugs there.'

I remember saying to the judge, 'Your Honour, this time I'm going straight when I'm released.'

He laughed and said, 'Go and see these people.'

When I got back to my flat, having done my time, it was clear that people had been using it as a dosshouse – windows were smashed, everything was gone, and needles were lying everywhere. I sat there with my best mate and demon, heroin, back to my old tricks. I forgot all about what the judge had said to me about that project called Havilah, until a lad called me up wanting to buy some gear.

I said, 'Where are you?'

'I'm down in the Havilah.'

Off I went to this place to meet a lad to sell him gear. Somehow I don't think that's what the judge meant when he told me to go there.

As I walked in I was met by a man called Jim – yes, the guy the judge had told me about. He pulled me aside for a chat.

'Listen, buddy,' he said. 'I know who you are and what you're here to do. I can't let you in here to sell drugs. We're here to help people, and if you want help then that's fine, you are welcome. But leave your drugs at home.'

I was stunned. This wasn't normal. Jim wasn't judging me or banning me or even phoning the police to say I was selling drugs in his drop-in. There was something different about this guy; I could see it in him. Here I was, doing the devil's work, selling a lad some gear, yet God had put someone in my path to grab my attention.

I started to go down the Havilah because they gave us food, and it was always a good place to see what was what.

A few weeks passed. Jim and his wife, Tracey, would speak to me; they would offer me help and told me about a place called Teen Challenge and how it helped people get off drugs. They often mentioned Jesus to me but never rammed 'religion' down my throat. Inside, I knew I needed to change, but I was stubborn. After a couple of months of them chipping away at me, though, I remember waking up, injecting into my groin, getting my morning fix, and looking round thinking, 'Is this what my life's come to? Living in a dump, smashed windows, nothing but a smelly sofa and a TV that doesn't work. Something needs to change. This isn't the dream I had for my life.'

I went down to the church and asked to speak to Jim and Tracey. 'This place you've been telling me about – I want to go,' I said.

They were shocked, but they replied, 'Let's do the forms!' I could see they were excited.

I knew something had broken inside me that day. At twenty-six I had had enough of this battle. I was feeling suicidal more days than I could count, and many times I had overdosed, but for some reason I had come round. I knew I had to change.

I went off to Teen Challenge in the Scottish Borders in November 2008. I will never forget my first few days there. It was freezing, and these mad Christians were standing in a chapel singing their hearts out to Jesus. Everything they spoke about was Jesus. I really didn't want to be there. I was withdrawing badly, and there was no detox, so I had to go cold turkey.

My room was next to the staff sleepover room, and all I could hear was this big loudmouth shouting his head off, laughing and joking around blasting-out crazy Christian music. His name was Paul. Little did I know that we would meet again later in life and become really good friends.

I remember one of these crazy nights in the chapel. They were all singing their songs, clapping their hands. It was December 2008. After the service, two staff members came up to me and asked if I wanted to give my life to Jesus. I said, 'I will give it a go.'

I started to repeat the prayer they asked me to say, and

suddenly I felt this peace come upon me. I could feel myself starting to smile for the first time in ages. I tried to hide it. I didn't want them thinking I was laughing at them.

'Go on, son,' they said. 'Smile – the joy of the Lord is upon you.' I was smiling from ear to ear by now. I felt different. I remember going to bed and feeling sleepy and thinking, 'This is strange!' You never sleep when withdrawing.

I stayed in Teen Challenge for three months. I had my first Christmas and New Year sober and drug-free – it was great. I felt I was ready to leave and face the world. I was out of rehab for three hours before meeting up with my brother and scoring some gear. Within days I was hooked again, but I knew something had changed inside of me. I didn't have the heart to rip people off any more. I would never have thought twice about it before.

'How am I going to make money to feed my habit now?' I thought.

I would make my little brother sit begging with me in Edinburgh. We could make good money doing that and we weren't committing crime. I was soon back to nine stone, living in a dirty house.

Jim and Tracey from the Havilah came and found me, and Tracey said, 'You may have given up on yourself, people may have given up on you and let you down in the past, but Jim and I aren't going to let you down. We are going to help you through this and do whatever it takes to get you clean. And what's more, God will never let you down.'

I went back to Teen Challenge, but this time in the northeast of Scotland. I did well there for a year and was beginning to plan my future. I wanted to serve God, things was looking up for me, and I just had to finish treatment for a blood disease I had. Then suddenly I cracked. I had a bit of history with one of the boys from Arbroath. I decided it would be a good idea to strangle him to show him who was boss. Sadly, I didn't feel like that a couple of hours later, sitting on the train having been kicked out for my actions.

Here I was, back to square one. I ended up at my brother's and we had a party for a few days before I called my mum. While I was in rehab, my mum had given her life to Jesus when she heard how Jesus had changed my life. And something life-changing had happened to her.

I went to stay with her. I joined the pipe band and managed to hide my heroin use for a short period of time. It was the summer of 2010. I had been playing with the band at the Glasgow world championships. I had been drinking all day and when I got home I decided to hit up some gear. The next thing I knew, paramedics were standing over me. My mum had found me overdosed with a needle hanging out of my groin.

For the next few days, I just thought about my mum. I knew exactly how she was feeling – just as I did when I found her overdosed when I was a child. I knew I had to get back into rehab, and quick.

I went back into Teen Challenge knowing that I had to get real with God. I wasn't there to muck around this time – it was life or death. I graduated in January 2011 and went off to Wales to their school of ministry before going back to work for Teen Challenge for a year.

I had 'met' Jesus in 2008, but I never really surrendered my life to him until 2010. It was then that I had a real encounter with him that changed my life forever. I felt a peace come over me – something that's hard to describe. I suddenly felt this calmness in the room and in my heart; the hairs were standing up on the back of my neck; I felt warm and full of joy.

In that moment I had no pain in my body from the withdrawals. I knew something different had happened to me. God set me free from drug addiction, healed me of all my hurts and pains, restored my family to me, and gave me a plan and purpose for my life. Everything I had been searching for all my life I finally found in Jesus – love, hope and acceptance. When I cried out to God for one last chance, I promised that I would serve him the rest of my days and go where he told me to go.

God has been so good to me and my family. I have seen many of them come to know the Lord. I met my amazing wife, Kirsty, in 2011. I had known who Kirsty was, as her mum worked in the Teen Challenge office, but I hadn't really spoken to Kirsty before, until New Year's Eve. I was working at Teen Challenge and we took the residents to the celebrations at King's Community Church in Aberdeen. We got chatting and I found out she had been a Christian all her life. After that, we spoke for hours on the phone and texted. I knew this was the woman for me; it was like she knew my heart. We shared a passion for Jesus and had a heart to reach the lost and make a difference in people's lives. She had been working with addicts in Rotherham, and I began to feel a calling to the community of Rotherham too. (My wife has now moved to an organisation that works with people rescued from human trafficking.)

When we got married, in 2014, Jim from the Havilah was one of my best men, along with that loudmouth Paul from my early days in rehab! Paul was the manager of the Solid Rock Café, an outreach café in the northeast of Scotland. He would often come into Teen Challenge to take chapel. We got to know each other the more he visited. He was a great encouragement to me and when I came back to work for Teen Challenge, our friendship began to grow. We would do a lot of outreach together and he helped me find my feet walking out this Christian walk. Paul and his wife are really good friends to my wife and I.

When I was an addict and first started attending church (more often than not, off my face), a man told me, 'God has great plans for your life. He's going to take you places you've never dreamed of.' At the time I thought he was crazy, but how true that statement was. I've had the great privilege of serving the Lord, preaching the gospel, and visiting some amazing countries on mission trips – Africa, Montenegro and the Philippines, to mention just a few. I felt a calling to reach addicts and prisoners, reaching out to the homeless in Rotherham with the Lighthouse. I have been there for four years now, and last year I took over as the manager.

I am part of the amazing Liberty Church in Rotherham, and oversee all the evangelism within the church. Recently I have been sent out to plant a church. I left school with no qualifications and last year managed to achieve a Level 3 Diploma in Health and Social Care, and in January 2016 I was accepted by the Assemblies of God Church to become a probationary minister.

I don't say these things to boast in myself, but simply to say, 'Look what Jesus can do.' Many people said I would amount to nothing. I thought I would end up dead by the time I was thirty. My family feared the worst. Many people said I would never get clean from drugs. I have reached out to some of those people over the last couple of years, giving them the same chance someone once gave me to change my life around.

Life is all about choices. One wrong choice could end your life, but one good choice could transform your life forever. I am thankful that there were people who never gave up on me – for Jim, for not judging me and giving me a chance of hope. But most of all I am grateful to God for rescuing me from a life of hell and giving me the ability to make the right choice.

7. PAUL & JULIE INNES

Paul

It was the summer of 1990 and I was eleven years old. I always looked up to my older brother and his friends and used to follow them around sometimes. One summer's evening I was with them and was stunned to find out that they were sniffing petrol. I remember the feeling of shock coming over me, as I knew how wrong and dangerous it was. Unfortunately, the shock soon wore off, and within a week I found myself sniffing my own bag of petrol. This was where it all began for me.

I was born and grew up in a fishing town called Fraserburgh, in the northeast of Scotland. I remember as a young lad I loved playing outside and was always on the go. We lived on a street called Ailsa Court. Everybody knew each other and there was a great sense of community spirit. I was the younger of two brothers, and growing up everything was great; Mum and Dad always worked very hard to make sure we had everything we needed. I remember as a kid looking forward to growing up, and had dreams and aspirations that got me excited.

I started sniffing petrol at the age of eleven and enjoyed the hallucinations and mad feeling that it gave me. Within a year I was smoking dope. The older brother of one of my friends was a heavy dope smoker, so we used to dip into his stash and get stoned. I remember lying on top of his bed smoking a joint with INXS's *Kick* playing loudly through the headphones I was wearing. I thought I was so cool! Little did I know that I was at the start of a downward spiral that would very nearly take my life.

The rave scene hit the northeast of Scotland in the early 1990s. I enjoyed the music and dabbled with ecstasy and speed, but wasn't too keen on the comedown afterwards. I was now smoking dope every day and started to take different tablets and downers.

I left school at the age of sixteen with no qualifications and no goals in life. The dreams I'd had when I was a child were no more; all I was interested in was getting stoned. I started a welding course at my local college and worked part-time in a fish factory. We used to get paid on a Friday and I would buy enough tablets for me and the guys that I worked with in the factory. I would sell them on to my friends at full price and in turn get my own for nothing. I remember going to my dealer one Friday afternoon to get my usual deal – a strip of Temgesic, and hash. My dealer told me that he didn't have any Temgesic but he did have 'smack' (heroin). I was apprehensive to start with, as I had never tried it, but I bought it anyway.

Heroin had only just landed in Fraserburgh and I didn't know many people who took it. I remember having to get somebody to help me take it, as I didn't have a clue how to 'chase the dragon'. The first time, I really enjoyed the way it made me feel; it gave me a confidence I had never known and was a high like I had never experienced. I started to buy smack every Friday instead of Temgesic, and within a matter of weeks I was totally hooked.

I remember the first time I experienced cold turkey. I felt absolutely awful and had a mad anxiety about me. I didn't know right away that it was withdrawals I was experiencing, but it soon dawned on me. I remember the shame of realising that I was a drug addict. This was never something I had set out to become. I made an appointment with my doctor and was put on a methadone prescription. Although this was supposed to help me come off heroin, it only made me worse. I now had two habits!

By this time I had left college and started working full-time in the fish factory. I worked hard and did a lot of overtime. The next ten years were a rollercoaster for me and my family. I lied, cheated and stole to feed my escalating addiction to heroin. I often found myself in situations where I promised myself I was finished with heroin – in a police station cell, desperate for a fix, having been caught with small amounts of heroin – but within half an hour of being released I was using. I remember sitting across the road from my best friend's flat, watching his body being taken out; he had overdosed and died. I told myself again that I was finished with heroin, but it had a grip on me that I was totally powerless to control.

My parents stood by me; they never gave up on me. By this time my brother was hooked on heroin as well. One night in April 2004 we were walking the streets of Fraserburgh sharing a bottle of Buckfast when we saw a poster for an event that was on in the leisure centre. A man called Nicky Cruz was speaking that night. The poster started like this: 'Ex notorious gang leader . . .' We decided to go to hear his story.

We entered the leisure centre and a man tried to usher us to a seat, but we said we were OK standing at the back. That night I enjoyed listening to Nicky's story, and there were some guys there from Teen Challenge Sunnybrae sharing their stories too – guys that I knew well and used to use heroin with. They were saying how much God had changed their lives and how they were no longer drug addicts. I was pleased for them, but didn't believe that God could do it for me. I thought I was too far gone.

My brother had started going to the Solid Rock Café (a Christian-run outreach) for help, and they were getting him a place in Sunnybrae. He invited me along to the café, but I told him I wanted nothing to do with Christians and the Church. I thought church was outdated and only existed for old people. But there was an American missions' team over at the café for two weeks, and my brother told me they were putting a meal on for the addicts of the town. I was sold! I met real, genuine people who cared. They told me how much they believed in me, and that God could change my life.

In September 2004 I lost my job at the fish factory and went even further downhill. I had a habit to feed, but no money. I would buy dihydrocodeine off the streets and self-prescribe. I tried different methods to get off the heroin. I did well for a couple of weeks at a time, but kept being drawn back to heroin.

By this time a place had become available for my brother at Sunnybrae, and off he went. By this time I was going along to the Solid Rock regularly, and they had all the time in the world for me. I met young men who were passionate about Jesus, and they would share stories from the Bible with me. I recall sitting upstairs in the counselling room with Daniel

Sutherland, a volunteer at the café. He shared the story of the Good Samaritan with me, but changed the story a little bit so that it was a Rangers fan helping a Celtic fan. He spoke to me in a language I understood.

Ben Ritchie, who ran the Solid Rock at the time, invited me along to church one Sunday evening on the promise of a fish supper afterwards. I was quite overwhelmed the first time I went. Everyone was very welcoming and I knew there was love in that place. I got the sense that the people there cared. I started to go along with Ben every Sunday evening and really enjoyed it. I would go along high and tanked up on Buckfast and heckle the preacher and protest when they played songs I didn't like!

I remember a couple from the church inviting me to their house one Sunday afternoon for dinner. I was blown away. Why would they invite a junkie like me round to their house for a meal? People were showing me love and it had a very real effect on me.

It was December 2004, and I had been up all night playing on my PlayStation. My friend rang me and told me he was on his way back from a very good fishing trip. He told me he would treat me to a day out and we would buy whatever drugs we could get our hands on. He picked me up in a taxi and we headed downtown and bought a load of tablets and were drinking Buckfast. By 2 o'clock that afternoon I was lying outside the shop I usually bought my Buckfast from, overdosed.

I woke up in Aberdeen hospital many hours later. I looked up and Ben and Dan from the Solid Rock were there. Ben told me I had been very lucky this time, but that might not be the case in the future. He chatted for a while, then, before praying for me, asked me if I had had enough yet. That question stayed with me over the next couple of days, and I thought about everything I'd had enough of. I'd had enough of hurting everyone who loved me; I'd had enough of waking up every morning, rattling; I'd had enough of struggling to get money together to score; I'd had enough!

The next couple of months were a bit more stable for me, but I had substituted the heroin and was smoking more dope and drinking more than ever before. I kidded myself that I was doing well!

It was 28 January 2005, I was in the Solid Rock and everybody was going home. Ben asked me to stay, as he wanted to talk to me. He told me that he felt it was time that I gave my life to Jesus. That night he led me in the prayer of salvation. It was absolutely incredible. Although nothing major happened outwardly, I felt excited and knew that things were about to change for me. I began to walk the streets of Fraserburgh telling everybody about Jesus. I was still on my prescription drugs, but I was excited about my Lord and Saviour, Jesus Christ.

There was a group of us that met up with the pastor of the church at the time, David Bizley. I am so thankful for his input in the early days of my journey. We would pray and do Bible studies together. I was speaking to my brother on the phone and I was encouraged at how well he was doing; he was telling me I had to go away to Teen Challenge and get totally clean. I wrestled with this thought but Ben was telling me the same thing.

I applied for Teen Challenge down in Wales. My methadone

was reduced and I entered the programme there on 19 April 2005. Ben and a man called Bob drove me down and I remember it all becoming very real to me as I said goodbye to them on the back step of Challenge House.

I remember my first chapel service. The worship was excellent and people were praying in tongues loudly (a prayer language that God gives to Christians that is mentioned in the Bible). I didn't know what to think! Had I made the right move? Would I stay and complete the full programme? I couldn't answer these questions, but decided to take one day at a time. Within three weeks I was detoxed and for the first time in fifteen years I was completely drug-free. It took a while for my head to balance out and for me to get used to my new-found freedom. I went through times when I thought I was off my head, but I also wondered if everybody else was off their heads!

The Teen Challenge programme was absolutely incredible, and I am so thankful for the ministry. It helped bring structure and discipline into my life, and was fundamental for me in growing in my relationship with God. I learned how to live life free from all the madness I had known in previous years.

On finishing the programme, I went on to the Teen Challenge school of ministry. This was a time of empowering and equipping. I loved my time there, and really enjoyed going out on the streets sharing my story and helping people who were in the same situation as I had been in. I felt called to the streets!

While I was at the school of ministry I made mistakes, but there was always someone there to cheer me on and help me face the challenges that were before me. I knew that no matter what, God was with me!

After the school of ministry, I went to work at a Teen Challenge centre in the Scottish Borders. I was able to help the men who were coming into the programme. It brought me a great sense of pride to see these men come to us broken and then leave with a sense of purpose and an excitement for life. I worked there for two years. I felt then it was time for me to go back to my home town. I always knew that eventually I would go back to Fraserburgh to help the lost and broken. I remember having a conversation with Ben Ritchie before I went away to Teen Challenge. I told him that one day I would be back home doing what he was doing.

In December 2008 I moved back home and started working at the Solid Rock. I had heard people speak about 'calling' and that sort of thing and I knew without a doubt that I had found mine! It wasn't long before I was taken on full-time, and within a year or two, I was in charge. I was in the place that I had come for help, and was now helping others . . . only Jesus!

I am still at the Solid Rock and my role is Community Chaplain. I love doing what I do. We have seen many lives transformed as a result of our ministry, and thank God for what he has done. Our mission statement is 'Providing drug prevention and cure in our schools, streets and prisons'. I go into the local prison every week and absolutely love it. It is an incredible privilege to do what I do, and I don't take it for granted. I am part of a great church and minister there regularly. I am currently pursuing my ministerial status with the Assemblies of God. I get the opportunity to speak in many of the local churches and have shared my story all over the country.

While I was at the school of ministry I met my wife, Julie. We married in September 2010 and have two children together. I now have a great relationship with my mum and dad. I'm so thankful for my new life and give God the glory.

I know that if God can do it for me, he can do it for anyone!

Julie

For eight years of my life addiction and chaos were normal for me; in and out of police cells, court appearances, long days filled with shoplifting, and dark nights on the street. How did my life get to this point?

When I was a child, I dreamed of growing up and doing something with my life. I wanted to get married and settle down, like most little girls do.

My mother and father got divorced when I was about five, and my mum tried her best for us. We had everything we needed, but it was difficult at times.

Things were good at primary school, then when I got to academy, it all began to change. I had an attitude and wanted to do things my way. Me and my friends would skip classes and smoke cannabis. We'd save up our lunch money for the weekends and buy bottles of cider. This was happening when I was twelve. I lost interest in school and was very rarely there. When it came to exams, I never put any effort in. I wasn't interested in getting good marks; all I wanted to do was hang out with my friends and drink and smoke.

I got into a relationship with a boy when I was thirteen, and I thought this was who I would spend the rest of my life with. The reality was I was still a child, and I didn't know what love really was. The relationship was rocky, but it was fine when we were taking drugs and getting high.

By the summer of 1997 we were taking ecstasy and amphetamines, and were out most weekends in nightclubs. I was underage but knew the places we could get into. I remember one night taking about ten ecstasy tablets. I was fourteen and thought it was great.

The next few years were just one big party until I left school at fifteen. I remember being introduced to heroin one night. We got it from a friend. I remember trying it and being really sick; heroin wasn't for me. I saw what people were like who took heroin. That wasn't what I wanted for my life – I just wanted to party and have fun.

Just before my sixteenth birthday I found out I was pregnant. I thought this would be great for me. We would be a family and settle down. My son was born eight weeks premature, weighing 4lb. I found life at this point all very hard to deal with. I felt helpless as I looked at my tiny baby boy.

While in the hospital, I was told that my boyfriend was addicted to heroin! I remember thinking that things would still be OK and we would cope with this, but shortly after we finally got our baby home, his dad went to prison. This just became normal for us.

I became very depressed and the doctor gave me antidepressants. I was struggling to cope, I wasn't sleeping, and I remember one night thinking about the time I tried heroin. I thought if I tried a bit again it would help me to sleep and settle, and it would just be a one-off.

Little did I know that it would control my life. I quickly

began taking it daily. It wasn't long before I needed this drug to function. I had become addicted.

My family noticed things weren't good with me, and my mum took me to the doctors. I was started on a methadone programme, and given sleeping tablets. I would go through spells of sticking to my methadone but then my partner would come out of prison and we would use heroin again. I hated having to go to the chemist every single day, rain or shine! I never imagined that I would ever live any other way.

Things were getting worse and I was shoplifting to fund my growing drug habit. I used to think I was invincible, but this was normally due to me being high. I would be shoplifting from the minute I woke up and felt the first shiver, and be at it all day. I would get greedy and this would result in another night in the cells. Some days it was impossible to get anything, due to me having to dodge the CCTV cameras if I had a warrant out for my arrest. Social workers were informed of my problem, which led to a whole other set of challenges. I couldn't seem to get a grip, although deep down I knew I wanted more for my life. I thought one day maybe I could stop using heroin and crack cocaine, but I had got used to the fact that I probably would always be on methadone.

Eventually, my son went to stay with a family member and I lost all motivation to change – even live. I really did hit rock bottom.

I was injecting daily and my body was in a mess. I had lost a lot of weight and struggled to walk due to abscesses in my feet and groin. I was smoking a lot of crack at this point, and my mind and physical health weren't in a good place. I would sit in my flat on my own and get high; my letterbox would clatter and I used to just sit and watch it, thinking people were trying to get in.

I was in despair and totally hopeless. I didn't really care if I lived or if my next fix was my last. Most nights, before I went to sleep I would cry, and then when I woke in the morning I would cry because I had to face this day doing the same old stuff and not seeing a way out of it.

Then I met some people who invited me along to King's Community Church, Aberdeen, and I remember for the first time in years feeling accepted and loved. These people went out of their way to help me; they would appear at my door most Sunday mornings to pick me up, and would often take me out for lunch during the week. I kept going back to church and within a few weeks I was introduced to someone who would help me turn my life around completely – that was Jesus.

I turned up at church one night in a mess. I listened to the sermon being spoken in between me gouching out (drowsing), and I remember my heart beating. Before I knew it I was up at the front, asking Jesus to forgive me and come into my life.

I left the church that night and nothing really changed. I still needed money for drugs. I went back to my flat in the early hours of the morning, and with my drugs and my crack pipe in front of me, I began to weep. I thought, just maybe there was another way of life, like the man had spoken about in church that night, so I began to ask Jesus to help me to change because I couldn't do it. I had tried and failed on many occasions. I had tried counsellors and drug treatment programmes but nothing worked for me; I always went back to what I knew. But that night something changed in my heart and I knew that if Jesus loved me and had a plan for me, then maybe I could sort my life out and get back all that I had lost. I began to have a little bit of hope.

The people from the church told me about a place called Teen Challenge and said I could go there to help sort my life out. Two weeks after my interview I was making the journey down to Wales. It was the start of the rest of my life!

The first day was a shock to the system. I was twenty-one and had a very bad attitude. How would I cope with structure and being told what to do? It was a struggle, but I soon realised that the attitude and hardness I had wasn't the real me. My lifestyle and poor choices had turned me into this person. I didn't know how else to be; I had to be hard to survive!

In my early days in Teen Challenge I was very ill during my withdrawal period, and ended up in hospital. I found out I had a bad strain of Hepatitis C, due to my years of injecting. Shortly after I completed the programme, I began treatment for this. Once I finished the treatment I was given the all-clear. However, after six months a test showed it had returned. This really shook me.

I was working full-time at this point and was excited about my future. I didn't know if I could face another twelve months of this horrendous treatment, but with the help and support of those around me – and more than anything the strength the Lord gave me to stick with it when it got tough – I got through it. I remember having a test done a year after I had finished and feeling so nervous. What if it happened again? Thankfully, it didn't. I had finally cleared the virus out of my body. They kept an eye on me for a while, but now I no longer have to be checked. I am thankful every day for my health.

I quickly discovered that God looked beyond my past and saw what I was to become. I remember the day that I really encountered Jesus for the first time. I was so overwhelmed with how much he loved me, despite all the stuff I'd done – the guilt, the heaviness I carried, was gone and I knew I was forgiven. I knew from that moment my life would never be the same and I would never be 'Julie, the heroin addict' again.

In the Bible it says, 'Therefore, if anyone is in Christ, the new creation has come: the old has gone, the new is here!' (2 Corinthians 5:17, NIV 2011) I was on a journey and in front of me was a clean sheet of paper. God had given me a new life. I had to learn how to live out my new life. I still had a lot of issues and things I had to overcome, but as I allowed God to lead my life, those things began to change. Hope was rising in me and I was beginning to dream again. The healing that came into my life was so powerful, but also very painful. I knew I had to let some stuff go if I wanted to move on in life.

God continues every day to amaze me with all that he has done in my life and the lives of those around me. He uses my worst circumstances to bring hope into someone else's situation. I work in a Teen Challenge centre in Scotland and on the outreach bus in Aberdeen on a Thursday night. I love seeing people come to know Jesus like I did all those years ago. My husband also came to Jesus through addiction and we serve him together. We have two young kids and my oldest boy is a teenager now. We have been so blessed and are forever grateful for the life we get to live.

8. JOHN EDWARDS

Mammy said Da was an alcoholic but I didn't believe her. He was the best da in the world and I would go out with him any chance I got. Sometimes we would go down along Dollymount beach to play golf at St Anne's Golf Club.

I had a stutter and it was getting worse.

'W-w-watch me p-p-putt-this one, Da.'

'Well done, son,' Da would say, even if I didn't do well.

I was left-handed from the time I was born. This was reckoned to be a bad thing in those days in Ireland. My father would say, 'John, you must learn to use your right hand for writing, and I am going to help you.'

One day he came home from work with a small black rubber ball. 'Here, John,' he said. 'Hold this in your left hand until you learn to use your right hand for everything.'

I remember being put out of the dining room when I would not use my right hand for my knife.

'Stand outside the door until you make your mind up to do as I say, John,' my da said. I would stand outside and cry. I began to fear my da.

The day I failed the secondary school entrance exam, something died in me. I lost the will to fight for myself. One summer day, me and my mates walked past a new crowd of young people. I quite clearly remember saying to the lads, 'I'm going over to get to know these people. See you later,' and I walked away from my childhood buddies. That decision was to change the whole course of my life.

I started hanging around with the new crowd. 'This is the life,' I thought. 'Having fun with my mates, going out with girls.' Yet deep down I was very frightened. My da's drinking had increased. My mother was on Valium antidepressant tablets because of the strain she was under, and they seemed to help her. I knew that I was depressed and needed help.

One day, while I was still only about thirteen, I stole one of her Valium tablets. Putting the pill on the end of my tongue, I drew it into my mouth, and a sense of calm began to steal over me. I had at last found something to help me and give me some rest from my inner turmoil. I continued to steal Valium from my ma's handbag and after a couple of weeks I needed two at a time to get the same effect, then three.

This was 1967; the drug scene was just beginning to hit Ireland. Our gang began to mix with an older bunch of lads from our neighbourhood. They were taking hard drugs, even injecting. We promised ourselves that we would never do that. We smoked hash, but we were in control and we would keep it that way. Yet we looked up to these guys; they were different and, as far as we were concerned, it was cool to get stoned.

One day in January of 1969, my teacher hit me, so I punched him back. On the following day, my da came with me to the school to meet with the headmaster. That was my schooling finished and I wasn't even sixteen. I was four months away from my intermediate exams, had no qualifications and was taking drugs and drinking too much. I was frightened of what the future held for me.

Da applied for a job for me at one of the top hairdressing salons in Dublin. I was now earning money. Not much, mind you, but the tips were good. I got enough in tips to live on.

My mates began to call round for me during the week. We would buy a few bottles of cider and some hash. I started going out with a girl called Susan. I met her at some stables, where we helped out with the horses sometimes. When the owner and his family moved out of the big house, a group of young people called the Children of God[1] moved in. They claimed to be born-again Christians and they seemed very happy. They didn't drink or take drugs, yet they were always smiling. The love of God seemed to shine out of them. Cormack, one of the leaders, prayed with me several times and I felt something like electricity move through me. I was left with a sense of peace deep inside. But then they moved on; I never found out where to.

At about the same time Susan told me she wanted to finish our relationship.

'I cannot go out with you as long as you're taking drugs, John,' she said. 'I really care for you but I am getting on with my life. Drugs are not going to be a part of it.'

The lifestyle surrounding drugs and alcohol abuse had a grip on me now. It was leading me down a very dangerous road and I was a willing captive.

On Saturday nights several of the gang travelled into Parnell Square in Dublin city. We got friendly with a girl called Liz. She always had lots of Valium and Mogadon, and sometimes she had barbiturates called Tuinal. She often gave me Valium and Mogadon. Less frequently she gave me Tuinal. These were very strong sleeping capsules. One or two of them would blow the head off me.

One night she said to me, 'Have you heard about the new drug centre that has opened up at the back of Jervis Street Hospital? I get my Valium and Mogadon there every week. I just told them I was getting flashbacks from acid and straight away they began to give me twenty-one blue Valium and seven Mogadon a week.'

I made an appointment at the drug centre. 'I'm getting f-flash-backs from taking acid, doctor,' I said, 'and I can't s-sleep properly as a result. I'm very anxious and panicky during the day as well. I was just w-wondering if there is anything that you could give me to h-help me.'

I walked out of there with twenty-one blue Valium and seven Mogadon sleeping tablets. I went back and did the same every week. This was really the beginning of my addiction.

One night, I lay unconscious in the shadows of a bus shelter. I don't know how long it was until finally a bus stopped. The bus conductor called to the driver for help and between the two of them they carried me onto the bus. They drove me straight to the A and E department of Jervis Street Hospital. I did not become conscious again until the following afternoon.

'Please God, if you're there, help me,' I cried to myself as I lay on my bed, all bandaged and stitched up. I was broken, inside and out.

My da came to see me in hospital. He gave me twenty cigarettes and began to plead with me to change my ways.

'I'll try, Da,' I promised.

He left the hospital that morning with tears in his eyes.

I got a very cool reception from my family when I returned to the house. My lifestyle was upsetting them. I made promises to try to stay off drugs, but as usual it wasn't long before I was back using again. I had promised myself I'd never inject. I knew that if I started to inject, there would be no going back for me.

One night, in a pub in Dublin, someone opened up to me and told me that he had begun shooting up his drugs. I asked him to give me an injection of Palfium. I could feel my legs shaking as we went upstairs.

'Fasten your seat belt, Johnny, you're going for a ride.'

With that he plunged the Palfium into my arm. Immediately I was caught up in the most amazing feeling I had ever had. I was as high as a kite.

In the 1970s, drugs were fairly easy to come by. Syringes were harder to come across. We sometimes shared one syringe between as many as ten of us for a couple of weeks. My health began to suffer at this time.

I never planned to get addicted; how could I be so stupid? Me, John Edwards, an addict! How could I do this to my mother? I told my parents that I intended to go into hospital to seek help. I was genuinely frightened. Was I losing my marbles? I wasn't sure about anything any more.

At the hospital, after I had been searched for drugs, they gave me a pair of striped pyjamas and an old hospital dressing gown to wear.

'I'll be off now, John,' my da said. 'Your mam and I will come in to see you tomorrow.'

He shook my hand. My da and I didn't hug any more. He was becoming like a stranger to me. Sometimes I didn't know what to say to him. I longed for him to be proud of me. I so much wanted to be his friend and to let him know that I loved him.

I managed to get hold of drugs while I was in hospital, and when I was discharged I came home to our house and made promises once again to my family that I would get my life together. I didn't tell them that I was already addicted to Valium again.

'God,' I cried inside. 'Why am I like I am? I cannot seem to take charge of my life and I'm hurting everyone that I care for.'

I decided to get out of Ireland and make a fresh start, so I asked my ma for a few quid to help me get over to London. I got the tube train from Euston Station to Piccadilly Circus in London's West End. I knew that I could get some drugs at Platform Four and sure enough, there was someone selling Tuinal barbiturates, three grain; five for a pound.

I made my way down to the Charing Cross Road and found a doorway to sleep in.

I heard someone say, 'Jesus loves you,' to a homeless guy. 'Nutter,' I said to myself. Then I thought, 'I've got some cheek, calling him a nutter! Anyway, God couldn't love me. Not after all I have done. He's finished with me.'

I didn't have enough money to get by. I spent the morning begging and made enough to do me for the day. I bought a syringe from a chemist.

I needed to find somewhere to stay and I got told about the Willesden Reception Centre. There were three or four men standing outside waiting to get into the centre for the night, but there were no rooms available. A black man approached us as we walked off. He had some leaflets in his hand.

'Here you are, boys,' he said. 'There's a Christian tent meeting on up in Willesden Park next week.' I took the leaflet and put it in my pocket next to my Tuinal.

'Maybe God is real?' Memories of the Children of God in Dublin came back to me. They were weird, but they were happy.

We walked on down the road to the off-licence and bought a few cans. I must have had a drug-and-drink-induced blackout then, because the next thing I remember is that I was in a pub; I can't even recall where it was. This English guy was promising me work the following morning. He bought me a half-pint of bitter and said, 'I'm going to the toilet. I'll be back in a few minutes.' I waited for about half an hour but he never came back. I put my hand in my pocket. My Tuinal was gone and so was my money. I had nothing left, except that bit of paper about the Christian meeting in Willesden next Saturday.

I was soon in withdrawal. Too sick to beg, I asked one of the dealers on Platform Four if he could sort me out with some Tuinal till later.

That night I shared a big dormitory with about twenty other men. The place was full of the stink of dirty socks, sweat, old clothes and stale booze breath. It was obnoxious. The bed linen itself was clean but I felt soiled just by being in that place. The next day I took my drugs and then I managed to get myself into the Willesden Reception Centre that night. This was a lot cleaner than the other hostel; everyone had to have a shower on the way in.

When Saturday came, I drank a bottle of cheap sherry and had a cocktail of drugs. In the evening I made my way up to the park and there I could see the tent, full of people praising God. There was a big, round pool on the stage that people were going to be baptised in. I was standing at the open door of the big tent, very stoned and drunk, but with something inside me wanting to go in. I marched boldly to the front, staggering a few times on the way. Some people managed to beat me to it. They climbed the steps in front of me and stood at the edge of the stage by the pool. Some of them were dressed in white gowns; I was in my dirty jeans and an old, worn jacket.

I stood there for ages. The preacher prayed with, and baptised, all the people in front of me, one by one, and even the ones behind me in the queue. Eventually, I was left standing on my own. I was beginning to feel stupid and very embarrassed. The preacher kept talking and completely ignored me. 'Maybe God doesn't want me,' I thought. 'Maybe I'm not good enough; even the Christians don't want to know me.' It was like I didn't exist and I cried bitter tears as I walked down the road.

I lived in a vicious circle of drug and drink abuse for about another year. Often I slept on the street. I had long hair and my weight was down to between seven and eight stone.

Sometimes I ate out of bins. I had also taken to drinking Jack, which is a mixture of surgical spirits and water. On two occasions I vomited up the lining of my stomach.

'Would you like a cup of tea and a sandwich, son?'

A woman and man in Salvation Army uniform stood there.

'Johnny,' David said as I chewed my sandwich, 'do you want

to get off the streets and get your life together?'

'You better believe I do,' I answered. 'I'm addicted to barbiturates, though, and Valium. I would n-need a lot of help coming off of them.'

'Well, Johnny, we have a couple of spare rooms in our house. You are welcome to use one of them until you get off drugs, but only so long as you go to a rehabilitation centre when you're clean from drugs.'

'OK, I'll d-do it,' I answered.

That night, I slept in a clean bed. I slept well but I was feeling a little sick. I had to take a barb to sort myself out. I only had two days' supply left and I was a bit worried that I might have serious withdrawals and convulse. I was terrified of the fits.

The withdrawals got worse and worse and I had to get out of the house. I knew a doctor who would give me barbs on tick and persuaded him to give me a prescription for thirty three-grain Tuinal. I was temporarily out of my sickness and withdrawals but I remember thinking to myself, 'If only there was a way of getting peace that wouldn't disappear.'

Four days later I woke up in the Intensive Care Unit of the Middlesex Hospital in London. The doctor told me that I had been in a coma for over three days.

'John,' he said. 'You need time to recover.'

'No,' I said, 'I want to leave.'

I lived like a rat on the streets for the next three weeks, begging for a living, staying in the shadows of London's West End and sleeping on cardboard in doorways and down dangerous alleys. I was threatened and beaten up. I managed to cut down on using barbs and took a lot of methadone amps and heroin. Heroin always made me sick and was never my first choice of drug, but I would use it when I could get nothing else. I was desperate. I could not take any more of living on the streets so I made my mind up I would go and ask David and his wife, Lorraine, to take me back. They did, and if ever I experienced unconditional love, it was at that moment.

From that time on in my life, I made a real effort to get better. I made my way to Harlesden in northwest London where I stayed in an old Irish dosshouse and began to attend Alcoholics Anonymous. I was still addicted to Valium, and I would spend most evenings out seeing doctors for it, but I was having a week here, two weeks there without drink. My self-esteem began to grow.

Then my sister phoned me at the dosshouse to tell me Da was dead.

'No,' I thought. 'He can't be. He can't die until I am well and he is proud of me and we're all friends again.'

'We all feel that it might be best if you didn't come home for the funeral. We are afraid that you might get stoned or drunk and upset Mammy. John, we all love you and want to see you, but. . .'

'It's OK, I understand,' I answered. 'That's part of my problem,' I thought to myself. 'I always understand.'

My da's death and the fact that I missed his funeral left a scar in my very soul. I needed drugs and drink to maintain my outer composure and calm the storms on the inside. I carried so much baggage of hurt, pain and rejection that I didn't know who I was any more. I lived in this state for a year before the compass of my heart began to point towards home. I needed my mother and I needed my family. I had nowhere else left to go. Thoughts of suicide were beginning to flash across my mind quite a lot in those days. I went around my various suppliers and got enough drugs to keep me going for a week or so when I got back to Ireland.

As I waited for the boat to dock in Dublin, I prayed. 'Please God, let my family accept me when I go home, and make me happy.'

Ma wasn't happy to see me, I could tell that. She looked at me without saying a word for what seemed like a long time before she said, 'You've caused me so much pain. I love you, though, and you can stay here with me.' She paused for a moment. 'But you'll have to get help for your addiction. You can't live here and keep drinking and drugging, OK?'

The next day I went about getting myself sorted out. I secured three prescriptions for Valium, enough to get me by. Then I signed on the dole.

One night my brother Michael came to visit me at my mother's. 'Hey, John, do you think you could do the Dublin Marathon this year?' He was putting out a challenge to me and I enjoyed that. I raised £500 sponsorship for the Irish Wheelchair Association.

I took several Valium before running the race and afterwards I went for a little drink to celebrate finishing. The next thing I knew, it was several days later. The £500 sponsorship money I had raised for the Irish Wheelchair Association was gone. I had spent the lot, so I had to borrow £500 from the Credit Union to pay the sponsorship money.

I was down and out again. I fell back on drink and drugs.

I came to myself one night in Dublin and hardly knew my name. I was dirty, smelly and very, very sick. I had had a serious blackout. I managed to make my way to a meeting of Alcoholics Anonymous in Killester in Dublin.

I observed these people for several months and got to know many of them. I discovered that they went to a Christian meeting in the Howth Lodge, a hotel on the north side of Dublin. I decided to go with them, but I was very nervous. Why would God help me, anyway? What had I ever done to deserve help from him?

That evening I felt a peace a bit like the peace I had experienced when I used to visit the Children of God as a teenager. I went to the next meeting. I needed God, if he was really there, to touch my life and change me. 'God, if you are the God that these people say you are, then please help me. You need to be so real to me that I can feel your presence every day.' I was crying now and pleading with God to come and reveal himself to me.

Suddenly, unexpectedly, it was as if the roof of the building burst off and the very hand of God came in and touched me on the top of my head. I could feel his power shooting straight down my body and something very evil leaving me. God was touching my life. I felt completely clean, forgiven and so very happy. God had just shown me that he was greater than any drug or drink.

I lived on this new experience for a few months, but I was still addicted to Valium. Every day I would have to go out and get my drugs. I always felt so guilty doing this, and when I had my drugs in me I would ask God to forgive me.

'John,' said Ellis, a man from the meeting. 'We are going to stick with you. God loves you, John, and so do we.'

I pulled myself together as best I could and soon managed to get a flat. One night I was reading the Bible, feeling desperate about my addiction, and I sensed the presence of God in the room.

Next morning was a Sunday, and one of the elders' wives at the meeting asked me to pray for her. 'What do you mean, pray for you?' I asked. 'Right now?'

'Yes. Lay your hands on my head and pray for me.'

So I did and I knew that the power of God was flowing through me. I prayed for many people after that. I even prayed for Bob, my old fighting partner who had chopped my ear in half, and his arm was healed. But I knew that I needed further help in my life. From time to time I was still falling back on drugs and drink. Some people said I couldn't be a Christian. Others said that I would never get my life together.

I decided to leave Dublin and go to Bible college in Galway, if they would have me. During my stay in Galway I got baptised. God was very real, yet I struggled with my studies and my nerves were clearly shattered from the years of drug-taking. One night I felt particularly desperate so I went to a doctor for a prescription for Valium. After taking them I got very drunk and had another blackout.

I regained consciousness in a part of Galway that I didn't recognise. I was wet right through to my skin and shaking like a leaf from the cold and withdrawals. I lay down in the straw in a horse box. When was this craziness going to stop? I had never felt so low before in my life.

'Horse,' I said, 'I'm giving in and going for some long-term help. If that doesn't work then I may as well just die.' I was ready to put my past behind me at last. 'Lord, into your hands I commit my life. Please set me free.'

When I arrived at Teen Challenge, a Christian rehabilitation centre in South Wales, I put my index finger through the wallpaper on the stairs; just at the corner where the paper had bubbled a bit and where it would not be noticed. I then promised myself that I would look at that little hole on the day I completed the programme.

The year of the Teen Challenge programme was the quickest and happiest year of my life up to that time. I was set free from cigarettes, drink and drugs on 10 April 1991. I faced all my problems of hurt and pain bit by bit. I talked them through and prayed them through and I began to lose my stutter. All the effects of my past were going one by one. On the day of my graduation, I put my finger into the hole that I had made in the wallpaper and I silently thanked God for setting me free.

I received an invitation from an American mission in London called Victory Outreach to work on the same streets that I used to sleep rough on. Many may think that going back to the streets was a crazy thing to do, but for me it was the high call of God.

'Excuse me,' said a tramp. 'Could you go into that shop there and buy me a can of cider? They won't serve me and I need a drink.'

'I will if you sit down with me for a while.'

He looked at me, no doubt surprised that I would spend time talking to him, and we both sat down on the cold ground to drink and talk.

I shared my life story and then prayed the Lord's Prayer with him. He repeated the words after me and I turned to look at him because the sincerity in his voice touched me. Tears were streaming down his face, coursing over the dried blood and into his dirty beard. 'John, I can feel a lovely feeling inside me. What's that?'

'That is God touching you,' I answered. His eyes were not dead anymore; instead, there was a glint in them, a glint of life; hope had come through a meeting with God. I knew then that he would never be the same again.

'God,' I prayed, as he walked away. 'Thank you for my life – it's been well worth it.'

1. The Children of God are a cult; John did not know this at the time.

9. LISA OYEBANDE

My life started out so secure. Born in Wembley, February 1966, we lived with my grandma (Bunny) in a house that had a great view of the old stadium with the twin towers. As a baby I was loved and cherished. I remember being taken out in my pushchair on to Wembley High Street, down into Alperton and over to Ealing; playing in Bunny's garden in the hot sun, listening to the trains rushing by beyond the fence; daring to pick apples that had fallen from the trees in the orchard. I didn't like that part of the garden, though. It was cold even when the sun was out, so I mostly stayed away.

Then we moved to Pudsey in West Yorkshire, to a one-up, one-down house. Mum was expecting my sister and things were a lot harder in the sixties. The house was very damp, so when Jayne, my sister, was a baby, we moved to a better house on a council estate in another part of Pudsey.

My dad was out of work – well, work you could talk about, anyway. He seemed to be around at some points and then disappeared. So when he did finally leave Mum and us, robbing the gas meter before he went back to London, I didn't really notice he had gone. When we were older we found out that he was involved in armed robberies and other crimes. When he wasn't hiding from others or the police, he was in jail. During a couple of rare conversations with him later in life, he gave his reasons for leaving. He said he just couldn't settle down anywhere. He had other children born before and after us. Yet, despite all of this, he was a really lovable character.

Grandad from Wales came to live with us. Grandad was hilarious and told us lots of stories from World War Two. He was Major John Mathias. He had come from a very wealthy family, but when he inherited the family fortune, he gambled it all away. We loved Grandad and he loved us. He probably drank, gambled and left us on our own too much when Mum was out at work, but he did his best.

Nana Lewis was more reliable. Every Friday she picked us up from school and took us back to her lovely bungalow, where our other grandad told us more stories of World War Two! We had fun weekends at Nana's. Once, to save water, Nana filled up the twin-tub washing machine and stuck us in there. 'Don't you dare tell anyone I bathed you in there,' she said. So funny. Nana taught us how to knit, bake and sew. We have never forgotten the times we had there. Especially the walnut chest of drawers in the little bedroom where we slept. The chest held a stack of white socks and clean vests for us.

After a while, Mum met someone new. He was a policeman and all the family were so pleased for her, probably because they thought she would be better off with someone like that. Grandad Mathias wasn't keen, though. One night, I woke up and heard Mum crying. Grandad was shouting, 'Get him out of here . . . something about him I don't like!' Then he started swearing in Welsh (I know that because he had taught us the words). A few more cross words were said over the next few months, then everything seemed to calm down. Mum eventually got married and we were little bridesmaids at the wedding. We moved away, just a few miles to a village nearby. Grandad moved into a ground-floor flat still in Pudsey but died of a heart attack shortly after. It was really sad.

As time went on, my new stepdad turned out to be too strict and very cruel. He started to abuse me physically and sexually. I was ten years old and the abuse went on for five years. Eventually I confided in a friend at school, who told one of the teachers. Everything snowballed from there and social services got involved. After giving a statement to the police I was taken into care, an assessment centre called Skircoat Lodge in Halifax. Mum didn't believe me and my sister about what he had done to me. We were on our own, whisked off that night in October 1981. I was fifteen years old. Jayne was thirteen.

Shortly afterwards, something happened that I couldn't comprehend and still struggle to understand today. Two detectives came to the children's home to talk to me about my statement. One of them, the one who did all the talking, said, 'Don't worry, Lisa, you're not in any trouble. Just sign this new statement. It says you were lying and that you're sorry.'

I couldn't speak. It was crazy; everything was upside down. Looking at my young social worker, who had tears in her eyes and was speechless, I stood up and screamed, 'No, I won't!' and ran out of the room. From that day on I just kept running.

Later that week I was found unconscious in the grounds of the children's home. I'd taken some pills, jumped out of a second-floor window and passed out. I was taken to hospital to have my stomach pumped. All I wanted was for everything to rewind back to the days with Nana in the bungalow, where it was safe.

My sister was missing our mum, and social services decided she would be going home for Christmas and staying there for good. I moved from Skircoat Lodge to another girls' home in Halifax and then on to foster parents. None of these places were permanent. I was lost and lonely. I was drinking and using glue. I just wanted something of my own to love. I wanted a baby. A baby girl.

A group of us who hung out at an amusement arcade called the Vodi in Halifax started to go over to Bradford, to a youth night at a club called Checkpoint. It was brilliant. We were all into Ska and the music they played was really good. I started going out with the DJ and, in 1985, our daughter, Jodie, was born. She was so beautiful; I couldn't stop staring at her. I couldn't believe she was mine. Nothing seemed to be going right, though. The relationship I was in was violent and I had to run. He too had his issues to face from a bad childhood. I left and went into a women's refuge.

By now I was smoking a lot of weed and had got into another relationship. One Saturday night, we had been out late. The next morning there was frantic knocking at the door. All I remember was a girl I'd never seen before appearing in the room. She ran over to me in the bed where I lay and kept punching me in the neck, stomach and arm. I stood up to push her off and felt something wet in my stomach area. It was blood. It was also running down my neck. Then I saw the knife on the floor. As the girl was tackled to the ground by two others, I realised I'd been stabbed repeatedly. It all happened so fast – seconds.

The ambulance was called and I had to have an operation called a laparotomy. It's a big operation; basically they take everything out and assess the damage. Mine was a punctured bowel, which meant I was being poisoned. During the operation, my left lung collapsed. The surgeon, J.J. Price (I still remember his name), said I made a miraculous recovery. I was very lucky; the wound to my neck was half an inch from my jugular vein. At the time it meant nothing, but later it meant the world to me. It meant my Father in heaven was watching over me.

I was still living at the women's refuge but Jodie's dad was angry about the relationship I was in and he took me to court for custody. It all looked really bad. My boyfriend was dealing drugs, I'd been stabbed and might be homeless because the refuge was for mothers and children. I lost the custody battle but fought to get Jodie back and won custody eighteen months later. I fell into depression and fixed it with drugs, weed and amphetamines. I suffered with panic attacks too.

A girl I knew took me up on to Lumb Lane, the red light area at the time in Bradford, and that's when I started working as a prostitute. The mind set I had was that I'd already been abused so at least I'd be paid for this. In reality, I hated myself. This went on for about eight years. Writing this now I'm wondering how I ever dared to do it.

The rave scene started and I went crazy. I loved the music, dancing, going to raves, travelling to Manchester and over to Liverpool to clubs. Gradually, the drugs got harder and heavier until I was smoking crack and heroin. At twenty-five,

I remember saying out loud to myself, 'Stop! What are you doing and where are you going?' It sounded like I was trying to tell myself off, but I wouldn't listen.

In 1992, Demi Rae, my youngest daughter, was born. We all loved her so much, she brought such joy to us and the people who were in my life at the time. Two of my close friends, even to this day, Lynne and Steph, were with me when I gave birth to her.

Demi's dad was on remand waiting for a big court case and I went off to Armley jail in Leeds on a prison visit. I had gone to a garage nearby and I bumped into a guy I knew from a pub up on Lumb Lane.

'Hi, how are you?' I said.

'Oh, hiya, Lisa, what you doing over here?'

'Just going on a visit.'

'I'm done with all that life now, Lis, I go to church and live over here in Leeds.'

'Yeah, I heard,' I said. 'Anyway, see ya.'

'Yeah, see ya, you take care now,' he said.

As I walked up to the prison gates, I started to think about Jesus and the times I'd prayed as a child in front of the Christmas tree. I thought about singing 'All Things Bright and Beautiful' at school. I'd always believed in Jesus and what he did on the cross – paying the penalty for everything we'd done wrong; it was instilled into us at school.

All I wanted was a normal life, but my record sheet was getting longer, so any chance of that was becoming impossible. It was one thing after another: court cases, road accidents, getting arrested. I forgot to sign bail once, so I paid a doctor

£10 for a sick note so I wouldn't have to go to prison. My life was crazy.

Sometime later, two students who lived on my street kept inviting me to church. They knew all about me and my troubles. To be honest, the whole street did. Jodie really wanted to go and she became a Christian when she was nine. She loved it and kept bringing me little cards she had made, with hearts and flowers and the words 'Jesus loves you' on them. She kept telling me, 'Everyone is praying for you, Mum.' She was so happy and I just thought how lovely it was for her. I had no idea how my life was about to completely change.

We were invited to an event for the weekend in Manchester. I thought I might as well go. Demi's dad was still in prison and I thought it was nice they cared and were praying for me. When I walked into the church, Yemi, still my good friend today, said, 'Oh, praise God! The gypsies are back.' I have dark curly hair and blue eyes, and there had been a big community of travellers recently attending the church. We still laugh about it now.

We sat down, then stood up and sang songs. My girls were happy. A man got up to speak and he cracked a few jokes during his talk. I did laugh and noticed that I hadn't laughed genuinely like that for a long time.

At the end of his talk he said, 'What you've got now, that's as good as it gets without Jesus.' The words went right into me. That statement hit me so hard, yet so gently. I thought, 'I don't have anything.' I'd just sold loads of stuff out of the house. With my head in my hands, I was thinking everything through. I'd lost my dignity, nearly lost my child, nearly lost my life. I didn't recognise myself anymore.

The man asked if anyone wanted to come to the front to pray. I wanted to know more and felt really drawn to what he was saying. I knelt down and a lady prayed with me. I was pouring out my whole life story and started to cry. I didn't stop crying for the next few hours, but it wasn't self-pity or as though I felt pain. It was relief, and the more I cried, the more relieved I felt. I prayed and asked God to forgive me for all my sins and for him to be Lord of my life.

An amazing miracle took place that evening. I no longer needed or wanted drugs. It's so hard to put into words what happened. I just know I emerged out of those tears a new woman. Something had replaced all those needs. It was the love of Christ. He filled my whole being up with himself. The next day was the same, and the next, and the next; no need or desire for drugs. The Lord helped me work through some massive insecurities I had and he continues to help me daily through difficult times. I now have my dignity. God's love and forgiveness has set me free. He has given me a new life. Some of that includes my husband, children and the work I do now.

In 1995, after becoming a Christian, I started going to the church in Bradford pioneered by Pastor Jonathan and Stephanie Davies from Manchester. We were there together for two years and I learned so much from them both. Their direction, love and care for me and my girls in those early days was crucial. We would visit the Manchester church every month, so I was aware of my future husband, Dele, even then. I knew him by name and to say hello to, but that was it.

In 1997, Pastor Jonathan had been praying and was going

to be moving back to Manchester to help out with the prison ministry. He asked me if I would like to move back with them. I don't think I let him finish his sentence before answering, 'Yes, I'm coming.' So off I went to Manchester. We hired a van and the pastors helped me move. Pastor Mike Aldaco had my two cats on his knee in the van as we drove down the motorway. He said to me, 'There are two things that I hate: prejudice and fur!' I assured him the cats wouldn't move. I'd put margarine on their paws as apparently it removes the scent so they can't find their way home. 'Sis, I don't think they will start running back up the M62,' he said. We all laughed so much during that trip and I knew that from then on we would have a blast.

And we did, for the next sixteen years. Someone should write about those years. In the Manchester church, I just ploughed into everything, keeping myself busy serving alongside Pastor Mike and his wife, Trini. Their wisdom and knowledge helped me to grow as a Christian. We were setting up a church school and I enrolled the girls into it. This is how I got to know Dele more; he was involved in educating the children there too.

I really felt like a young girl again – you know, that funny feeling when he walks in the room – but I had to keep it to myself. I could see there were others who liked him and at the time I wasn't sure how he felt. I also had mixed emotions about myself. The others were younger than me and probably weren't scarred like me, mentally or physically. But all these negative thoughts soon went away after spending time with Dele. We talked about anything and everything. He made me feel like a real person who had something to offer. He was interested in what I had to say, and valued my opinion. One friend said,

'You bring the best out in each other.' He was a total gentlemen – still is. We remained friends for the next four years, getting to know one another and working alongside each other in the school and in church. It was obvious to everyone else how we felt, yet we never told one another, never spoke it out. It all felt a bit Pride and Prejudice! What I mean by that is it was pure, old-fashioned dating. I loved it.

There wasn't any rush and we both knew to be patient. Dele also had some opposition because of his cultural background, which was Nigerian. Then, in October 2000, Dele proposed and we were married in March 2001. I walked down the aisle, on my own, to a piece of music called 'Give Me a Smile', written by John Barry. I felt so peaceful that day and really honoured. Not because this man who had a PhD had married me, but because he saw past all of my past. He called me his rough-cut diamond. I think I may still be a bit rough round the edges, but I am a work in progress. Jodie and Demi were bridesmaids at our wedding. Their relationship with Dele grew naturally and that was the best way. He has been a great influence in their lives and we continue to be a close family. In addition to the girls, we now have two boys, Benjamin and Lewis.

We started attending the Lighthouse Church in 2013, led by Pastor Paul and Mags Hallam. They and the rest of the leadership team have really supported and loved us from the moment we stepped into the church. It's as though we have known them all our lives. At the Lighthouse, you're totally supported and encouraged in your ideas, dreams, visions, whatever you want to call it. You're listened to and encouraged. Dele and I started to run a life group from our home during the week and are involved in a number of other ministries within the church. In 2015, I set up an outreach ministry called Street Level, reaching out to women on the streets who may be struggling with addiction and poverty. We became affiliates with Beyond the Streets. They are an amazing organisation that provide training, support and awareness of on/off street prostitution. A friend also mentioned the possibility of obtaining some funding from a Christian charity, which we applied for and were happy to receive.

As a team, we at Street Level are still developing the vision. We support women by bringing them food, helping them with prison visits, standing with them and their families in court. A lot of what we see and hear is heartbreaking and I can see that women working on the streets today have different challenges. I know that it is possible for them to change and, with God, all things are possible. Look what he did in my life. This is what drives me every week to reach out to the women. One thing we do know is that it's going to be a long-term project.

My co-worker, Tina, is a nurse and passionate about what we do. She said a few months ago, 'Which one of these women when they were little girls ever dreamed of becoming a prostitute? None.'

More recently, I have been privileged to be mentored by Barry Woodward via his Evangelist Network and other events. The training here has been immense and I will treasure it. Also, Alison Fenning, a great speaker, has provided valuable coaching and opportunities to share my story. Another opportunity came just this week, while writing the end of this, to go into Styal Prison and share my story. There are plans to have an outreach there every Monday.

If all of this helps just one person, it will be worth it.

I'm also a nana now, making sure my little grandchildren have white socks and clean vests!

10. ROD WILLIAMS

'What I have done this time?' I thought to myself as I woke up in the custody suite of the police station. My head was battered from whatever cocktail of drugs and alcohol I had taken the previous night. I couldn't remember much at all, although I knew it must have been bad.

I had only been out on parole for six weeks. I was given a four-year stretch for drug trafficking offences in Guernsey and had only just got my first parole for good behaviour. I started to have flashbacks from the night before. I couldn't believe it. No, not again! I recalled something of a car chase with the police that resulted in a roadblock being put out to stop me. The events of the night before became clearer after I was taken for interview and was told that after being stopped and arrested on suspicion of drink-driving, I had escaped police custody and driven off. This resulted in a fifteen-minute high speed police chase around the island, where the maximum speed limits are between twenty-five and thirty-five miles per hour. Apparently it was one of the worst cases of dangerous driving ever known on the island.

I knew this would mean my parole licence being revoked and me going back to prison. I felt sick. What were my family going to say, after all they had done in supporting me through the last time? What about God? I had been a Christian for just over twelve months, after an incredible encounter with God in my prison cell one night. Surely I had gone too far this time for God to give me a second chance?

I grew up in Swansea, South Wales. Both my parents worked for the police. My dad was an inspector. My mum and dad were Christians and we regularly attended church. My sister and I were taught Christian values from a young age. To be honest, though, church never really interested me. I didn't get what it was all about. I do remember some lovely people in the church who were very kind to us, especially to my mum after she and my dad separated and later divorced.

When I was ten, we moved to Guernsey in the Channel Islands after Mum remarried. Moving to an island some call a millionaire's paradise with low unemployment and a low crime rate, it created the best opportunity that I could have possibly had to progress well in life. My stepdad was a Christian too and going to church was just as important to him as it was to my mum.

After getting good grades in high school and gaining a business studies qualification at college at eighteen, I began a career in the finance industry. I was happy, my parents were proud, and my future looked bright.

What my parents didn't know was around this time I had started to experiment with drugs, mainly smoking weed with my new friends who I had met at college. It was just a bit of fun at weekends, not doing anybody any harm. That's what I thought, anyway.

I was earning a nice wage for my age. It meant I had more money available to spend on the wrong things. I entered the club scene and was introduced to ecstasy and amphetamines. I enjoyed the buzz the drugs gave me. Getting off my face on ecstasy was the one thing I looked forward to all week. I was meeting new people and making new friends – this included drug dealers. I could see there was serious money to be made from selling drugs, especially in Guernsey where prices were between five and ten times higher than anywhere else. So when one night I was offered a bag of ecstasy tablets to sell, I took them on knowing they would all go in no time. They did.

Following that night, it would be a rare occasion if I didn't have some kind of illegal substance to sell. That decision to sell drugs took me into a world that promised me everything – power, pleasure, popularity. It felt good walking into the pubs and clubs with a constant flow of people coming up to me wanting me to sort them out. It felt good walking around with bundles of notes in my pockets. It felt good watching people on the dance floor off their heads enjoying themselves because of what I had given them. I thought I was invincible; I didn't think the police would suspect an innocent-looking bank worker of doing what I was doing.

I was making a nice sum of money, but I was never satisfied. I always wanted more. My pursuit for more took me into the bookies one day where I placed a £5 bet on a horse. That £5 would end up turning into around £100,000 that I ended up losing over the following six years. Every spare minute of the day, when I could, I would be in the bookies betting on anything and everything that moved. Gambling addiction had such a strong hold on my life it had total control over me. I would come up with systems to try to beat the bookies but they never worked out, the bookies always won – they always do. I got used to the sick feeling in my stomach after losing my wages on payday – sometimes in a couple of hours. It was the same with the profits I was making from the drugs. It was only a matter of time before I would get in debt with my supplier. I would risk using his money to gamble with, convincing myself I would win back what I had lost and still be able to pay my debt. Even on the few occasions this did happen I would almost immediately blow it all again. I would have to think of ways to get the money back, such as bank loans, credit cards, scam my family out of money somehow, or take on more drugs to sell – I did all of this.

My family became suspicious of my behaviour. They saw the change in my character and they were concerned. They had heard rumours of what I had been doing – it doesn't take long for rumours to go around a small island. My dad flew over to the island on more than one occasion to talk to me. He told me that I was causing the family worry and distress and warned me that there would be severe consequences if I didn't stop what I was doing. I denied everything. I wasn't ready to stop until I made it big.

By my early twenties I was involved in smuggling drugs into the island as I saw this was where the big money was. After a couple of successful attempts, things started to go horribly wrong. People were getting arrested bringing the drugs over, and being sent down for a long time. I felt guilty about being involved in something that was robbing people of their freedom, including good friends of mine. I had been arrested too, but there was no hard evidence to convict me. My parents' house was raided on a few occasions but nothing ever found. This devastated my mum, who was sick with worry by now.

The police were on to me big-time. I became a paranoid mess. Everywhere I went I thought I was being followed by undercover officers. I was always looking over my shoulder.

At twenty-two I couldn't deny my involvement with drugs any longer. I was busted in a local club with two ecstasy tablets and some weed. I was fined £1,300 and named and shamed in the local paper. My boss was very gracious and allowed me to keep my job in the bank, giving me a second chance.

By now, my head was in bits. I was caught in a web of crime and addiction that was destroying me. This life that had promised me everything was actually robbing me of my life. To my friends I wore my 'got it all together' mask, but inside I was hurting, I was depressed, I was lonely. Addiction will always take you to the lowest common denominator, and that is where I was heading.

I became addicted to heroin when I was twenty-three after 'chasing the dragon' and finding comfort in the way it helped me to escape reality. It numbed all the pain that was going on inside. I had seen heroin destroy lives all around me and now it was destroying me. Within twelve months I lost everything, including my job and my house. In a desperate attempt to try to sort myself out, in December 2001 I went to live in Thailand, but only lasted two months. I became addicted to methamphetamine. This played havoc with my mental health and I could see (and others could too) that I was on the verge of losing the plot. After returning, I was back on the 'brown' and started on crack cocaine too. I spent long periods of time in a crack house in Brixton, London, where I was surrounded by other addicts.

In March 2002 I decided enough was enough. I wanted out. I couldn't cope with this lifestyle any longer. There was one problem, though. I still owed a drug debt and 'Mr Big' in Guernsey had lost patience with waiting. He threatened my life and my family's too if I didn't pay the debt within a week. Gripped with fear, and after some time contemplating and thinking of ways to get his money, I decided the only way was to do the dirty work myself and carry enough heroin and crack into the island to pay the debt. I had planned to sell the drugs, pay what I owed and get out completely. I was serious. I wanted my life back. I wanted my family back. This was the only way, I thought, that would make this happen.

This journey that was supposed to be a journey to freedom ended up being a journey to imprisonment. I was busted at Guernsey Airport. The drugs were found. I was headed to prison.

I was looking at four to six years. How was I going to cope? I had never done jail before. Plus, I was going through withdrawals. I was put on F Wing. I saw a lot of familiar faces; they were all my mates from the 'out'. They seemed happy to see me and gave me a warm welcome, as if I had done something good. I find that strange, on reflection. They sorted me out with baccy and phone cards straight away. This meant I was able to phone my mum and dad to tell them I was OK and to say sorry. They were difficult phone calls to make, but I knew I had to do it. I'll never forget the love and grace shown to me after everything I had done and put them through. Especially Mum, who believed wholeheartedly that there was going to be a better day for her son – and she told me that many times. Mum said she was praying for me; I knew she would be, as was my whole family. My dad had people praying for me all over the world from his connection with the Christian Police Association.

Being in prison gave me a lot of time to think about the life I had been living, and there was a genuine desire in my heart to want to change. I started to read testimony books of transformed lives that my parents had sent me. These were inspiring; emotional too. I was reading about gang members, drug addicts, prostitutes, and how their lives had been radically changed after an encounter with Jesus Christ. Something was stirring in my heart and I couldn't wait to pick up the next book to read more of these miraculous stories.

This got me thinking about everything I had heard in church growing up about Jesus dying on the cross for me so that I could receive forgiveness for my sins and have eternal life. Admitting my sin wasn't an issue, but I had trouble believing that forgiveness was available for me. I believed in a heaven and a hell, and the thought of spending even a minute in hell filled my heart with fear. It was three months into my sentence when I decided to put myself right with God. I got down on my cell floor and began to speak to God, saying sorry for everything I had done wrong, and asking him for his forgiveness. I can't remember the exact words, but there were a lot of sorrys and tears. That night I knew how real God was. My prayer was answered. My heart was filled with a love I had not known before and a peace I had been searching for all my life. I felt forgiven. Nobody could have convinced me that what I was experiencing wasn't real. I had hope for the first time. I knew that God had a plan for my life, and even though I still had a couple of years of my sentence to do, I was excited about my future.

I wrote letters to Mum and Dad, telling them what had happened. When they realised I was serious they were ecstatic – their prayers had been answered. I'm so glad that they never gave up on me. From that night I began to talk to God and read the Bible. Even though there was no audible voice, I knew he was with me and talking to me through His Word. I began to see answers to prayer, and I don't believe they were just 'coincidences'. I believe it was God showing me how real he was.

I was now on a journey with my Saviour Jesus by my side, and it felt good. What could go wrong for me now?

Well – I think it's important to be real and tell it like it was. I still had choices to make and would continue to make some pretty lousy ones at times. After getting my first parole for good behaviour and rejecting the advice from my parents to go on a Christian rehab programme, it wasn't long after my release that I began to gravitate back to the old places and began meeting up with old friends.

I was only out for six weeks before having my parole licence revoked for committing further criminal offences. I had taken a cocktail of prescription drugs and alcohol, and ended up being arrested and escaping police custody that resulted in the high speed chase around the narrow lanes of Guernsey I mentioned at the beginning of my story. I was now heading back to prison to finish my sentence. Surely I had gone too far this time for God to give me a second chance?

God's response to me wasn't condemnation. He didn't point the finger but he saturated me with his love, mercy and grace, and gave me a second chance. I did end up going to Christian rehab (the Lighthouse Foundation in Widnes, Cheshire) after the parole board agreed to release me on parole for the second time – something they had never done before or done since. God was on my side. It was 1 June 2004 when I walked through the door of the Lighthouse, and that is the day I nailed my colours to the mast, giving God everything. I have not looked back since that day.

I was on the programme, which was tailored to my needs, for sixteen months. A platform was created for me to rebuild my life on a solid foundation of nothing else but Jesus Christ. The staff there were overflowing with passion and love for God – it was contagious. I wanted what I saw in them. I became passionate, with a strong desire in my heart to reach other people with the same gospel message that was changing me. Following my graduation, I began to work there full-time as a support worker – a job I held for four years. What a privilege it was to serve God by helping others who were broken in their addiction. It was ironic that two of the students who came on the programme when I was working there were my old friends. They saw the change in me and wanted it themselves. These were the same people I was gambling, dealing and smuggling drugs with only a few years before. I was now their support worker. They both became Christians and their lives were turned around. Nobody turns around messy situations quite like God. He is amazing.

So now as I was putting God first in my life I was seeing an acceleration of his kindness and favour. In November 2005, I started dating a girl I had met at the church I was attending at the time. Her name was Kate. Kate had brown shoulder-length hair, piercing blue eyes and a pretty smile. Kate shared the same love for God and for people that I had. I couldn't have asked for a more perfect girlfriend. We are now coming up to ten years of married life.

I saw God restore relationships that had been broken. I experienced healing and freedom from my addictions. I was given responsibilities by my church leader that not many people would have given to an ex-addict/criminal. Having people around me who believed in me and trusted me made a big difference. There was no way I was going to let them down.

One of my responsibilities at the church was to manage the Christians Against Poverty (CAP) debt centre, which I did for five years. I was also a chaplain for a group of elderly people who lived on the church site. During that time I saw God do incredible things, especially through the debt centre. We saw over forty of our clients come to faith as they saw love in action. This fuelled the passion in my heart to see more souls saved, and God opened the door for me to share my story from the platform and preach the gospel. There was no greater buzz than seeing people respond to God at these meetings. I now get to travel around the country for CAP speaking at outreach events, seeing the power of the gospel change people's lives. I have also written an autobiography called *The Real Deal*

(Authentic, 2014) and get to speak in prisons offering hope and healing.

If somebody had told me fourteen years ago that my life would be as it is now, I don't think I would have believed them. I thought I was disqualified from having my life back because of the things I had done. I thought I was disqualified from being given a second chance by God. You may be reading this thinking exactly the same thing. I hope you have seen from my story that this wasn't the case, and it's not for you, either. Remember, it is God's unconditional love that qualifies the disqualified, and there is absolutely nothing that can separate you from his love.

II. BARRY WOODWARD

It was the eighties and I was living on William Kent Crescent in Hulme, Moss Side, Manchester in the UK. I got busted. The charge was possession of heroin, with intent to supply. But because I had lots of other charges, I didn't get bail. I got taken to Strangeways prison on remand. This wasn't my first time in Strangeways. Because I was an addict they put me on the hospital wing, and then I was put on K-wing in a cell with a guy called Lennie.

Lennie was from Glasgow. He was about five foot six tall, he had a humped back, he had ginger hair, he had a ginger beard, his moustache hung over his lip, his hands were brown with smoking Old Holborn roll-ups so short. And he stunk of tobacco.

Lennie had just done five years for manslaughter. The first thing he did after he'd been released was, he went round to the judge's house who had given him the sentence and he broke in. His reason for being there was to kill the judge but the judge wasn't in. So Lennie wrecked his house and slashed his clothes instead. Lennie got caught and he got put back in Strangeways, on remand.

So here I was, sat in a cell with Lennie from Glasgow. We got on really well.

I was an addict and being in prison wasn't going to stop me

getting my drugs. At the time, I was going out with a woman called Lisa and she would come to visit me every day she could. You couldn't have a visit on a Sunday so Lisa came six days a week. She would get all the prescription drugs that we used to use – we had different doctors that we'd get them from. Lisa used to buy the heroin, put it in a condom and tie it in knot so it was in a little ball. Then she'd put it in her mouth and come to prison to visit me. She'd walk through the prison gates and into the visiting room, where there was a big long table with a divider down the middle. At the end of the table there was a prison officer sat watching down the divider. Lisa would sit on her side of the divider and I would come out and sit on my side. You weren't supposed to have any physical contact.

After my visit, I'd stand up and reach my head over the divider. Lisa would meet me halfway and she'd kiss me, put her tongue in my mouth and she'd pass the drugs across. I'd lodge the drugs in my throat, and then I'd walk through the prison system after being searched. And they didn't find a thing. I did that day in, day out.

Lennie wasn't really into drugs. He was more of a boozer, but he'd take anything to get off his head. So we used to smoke a bit of heroin together because we didn't have a 'works'. I used to inject at the time. We didn't have any needles and syringes, but then I discovered that the guy who was in the next cell to me, Spike, was a heroin addict. He'd smuggled in some needles and syringes; his girlfriend used to come in and visit him every day.

Spike's pad mate got bail so I got permission to move in with Spike. We got our visits every day, we'd use our drugs and we were OK.

I remember it was a Saturday and we were lying on our beds. Usually, Saturday in prison is a busy day – a lot of people get visits – so there's a lot of noise. You can hear the prison officers walking up and down the landing, and you can hear their keys jangling, and you can hear the chains jangling, and the keys going in the door. You can hear the clunk-clicks of the doors opening and closing, you can hear the cons speaking to each other . . . But on this particular Saturday it was really quiet. I'm lying there on my bed, Spike is on his bed.

I said, 'Spike.'

'What?'

'Isn't it quiet today for a Saturday?'

'It must be just a quiet day.'

I thought, 'Fine,' and I heard the key go in the door. 'It's time for my visit, time to get my drugs for the day.'

The door opened and a sniffer dog came in – four or five prison officers as well. 'Right, lads, stand up. Put your arms in the air. You're being busted.'

'What do you mean, boss? What do you mean, we're being busted? We've done nothing,' we said. I was standing there with track marks all the way up my arms.

We got busted. It was a Saturday and they put us in solitary confinement. Lisa got kicked out of the prison. She denied bringing in drugs. When she came to visit me, she came just after they'd busted us so she was able to swallow the drugs and use them herself.

So on the Monday, after we'd been in solitary confinement on Saturday, Sunday and Monday, we had to go and stand before the governor. We'd been caught in prison and they'd found needles and syringes and all the paraphernalia you needed. We lost five week's remission, and we got sent back to the block for five weeks.

What's it like in the block? Well, the block is an empty cell. In the daytime you can have a cardboard chair, a cardboard table and you've got a steel-framed bed with no mattress on it. In the corner of the cell you've got a bucket – not for washing in – and on the other side of the cell you've got a container that has some water in it. That's all you can have in your cell. At 6.30 at night you take out your cardboard chair and your cardboard table. You bring in your mattress and you put it on your steel-framed bed. The next morning when you get up, you take your mattress out and you bring in your cardboard chair and your cardboard table.

I remember going through withdrawals in solitary confinement. My back was aching, my legs were aching, I was hallucinating.

Every now and again one of the screws would come past my spyhole and shout something in, just to wind me up.

When you're in solitary confinement you can't have any open visits. I could still get a visit from Lisa but now I was on closed visits. There was some Perspex between us, so I couldn't get the drugs that I was used to. I went through major cold turkey in solitary confinement.

But let me take you right back to the beginning.

My start in life was good. I was born in Salford, Greater Manchester. I had two great parents. I went to primary school like everybody else, then I went to secondary school. I really struggled doing the stuff that the teachers asked me to do at secondary school. I couldn't get my head around any of it so I'd sit behind the clever ones and copy them. I left school at the age of sixteen. I took two exams and I didn't even go back for the results, because I knew I'd failed.

Soon after leaving school I met some lads who were using drugs. Smoking weed, cannabis, taking LSD, using amphetamines. As a young person, I was really curious. I wondered how these drugs would make me feel, so I started to hang around with this group and then I started using the drugs with them.

There was this particular pub in Manchester called the Union and it was a right dive back then, but we liked it in there, because the manager let you smoke weed, just as long as you sorted him out. And so we'd go there, smoke draw all night and then go into the clubs.

There was a woman who used to come in to the pub who used to deal drugs for a Rastafarian who lived in Hulme, Moss Side. She was eleven years older than me and her name was Lisa.

Lisa used to come out, she used to do the business – smoke the draw, sell the drugs – and then she'd go home and give her profits to this Rasta.

One night she looked over to me and she smiled. The kind of smile that says, 'This girl fancies me.' I smiled back. I thought, 'She's a bit different.' And I knew that she was dealing drugs for this Rasta.

That night we went to a nightclub and Lisa was there. She really was after me, so I took her home that night, gave her a bit of a kiss. And then the next night I saw her again. I started a relationship with her while she was going out with this Rasta.

By this time, I was losing contact with all of my friends that I had in Salford because I was going to Manchester every night. Lisa lived in Hulme. Eventually there was a confrontation between us and Lisa left the Rasta.

Lisa and I started to sub-let a flat and I left my job in car valeting because I realised that I could make more money dealing drugs. I sold weed, amphetamine, then eventually started dealing heroin.

I had a nice flat. I had nice furniture. I had a top of the range hi-fi. I had a nice car. I had nice clothes. I had jewellery. Lisa had jewellery. We had everything we thought was important – and then I got nicked.

They wouldn't give me bail and I was put in Strangeways for the very first time. I was on G wing, the young offenders' wing. As soon as I got out from Strangeways I went back to Hulme, wheeling and dealing. Then I got nicked again. And again. Back into prison, out, wheeling and dealing, back into prison.

I remember being released from Preston prison once. Lisa was waiting for me at the gate and she had some weed with her. Oh, I was so excited about being out. We walked through Preston to the train station, smoking weed.

'Lisa . . .' I said.

'What?'

'We're going to go on a bender. I've been locked up for too long. We're going to go on a big, big bender.'

So the train took us to Manchester, then we got a taxi from

the train station back to Hulme and we started this drugs marathon. We went to doctors to get our Valium, DF118s and methadone. This was easier to get by now and we bought loads of amphetamines and started this bender – a bender that lasted nine months.

I wouldn't let myself sleep. I was into house music. It was about 1986 and all this music was coming over from America. I was recording it from pirate radio stations. 'I love this music!' I got a little drum machine. I got a synthesiser and a keyboard, and I started to make all these different noises. I made this repetitious house music and all the while I was off my head on amphetamines and all these other drugs.

Then after nine months, right out of the blue, I started to hear voices. Real evil, horrible, aggressive voices. You think of the worst language, in the worst tone, and it was worse than that.

I said to Lisa, 'Can you hear those voices?'

'I can't, Barry. They're all in your head.'

I said, 'Don't you tell me they're all in my head. Can't you hear those people shouting out at me?'

'No.'

'Don't you tell me you can't hear them. You're part of it, aren't you? You're planning against me.'

I went to see my doctor. This is the only time I went to see a doctor for a genuine reason in those days. I said, 'Doctor, I'm hearing these voices. They're horrific.' So he referred me to see a psychiatrist, who sent me to Cheadle Royal Psychiatric Unit in Manchester. Hearing these voices was the lowest part of my life. They were constant, 24/7, and they didn't go away.

Eventually I was released from that psychiatric unit and I moved back to Moss Side.

After a few weeks we got an exchange, and we moved out into the sticks into Heywood – Darnhill, into this high-rise flat on the seventh floor. Me, Lisa and the voices.

Time passed. Lisa and me split up. Then after fifteen years of hard-core drug use and addiction, a string of broken relationships, living in various parts of Manchester, I moved to Rochdale on the outskirts of Manchester. I was in a Salvation Army hostel but I got kicked out for beating up this guy from Liverpool. He was a young kid and he was always picking on the old people. My dad brought me up to respect my elders, but this kid was always ripping them off and laughing at them.

One afternoon he was playing his music. He was on the same corridor as me, and I was in my room. I went out and said to him, 'Turn your music down, mate.' I went back into my room and he turned it up. I went out again and said, 'Turn your music down, mate, please!' I went back in my room and he turned his music up.

Listen, I wasn't really a fighter, but if it kicked off I could handle myself. So there I was in my room thinking, 'I can't handle this!' and I snapped. I went out of my room and I smashed his head in, I smashed his room up and he grassed me up. So I got kicked out, and I ended up in Leopold Court hostel for a couple of weeks.

But then I got an offer of a flat. Not council, housing association. I picked the keys up and I went to see it. Down a cul-de-sac, it was, PVC windows, first floor. It had a view of a football field. Oh, it was wonderful and I thought, 'I'm going to take it.'

I was living on my own, just me and my dog. I got a little dog from Harpurhey Dogs' Home, a little Jack Russell, and I called her Kim. I was using all my prescription drugs – my methadone, my Valium, my DF118s, and smoking weed. I did take some speed, but not a lot because I couldn't handle a lot of it since my breakdown.

I was content. I got my grants from the social. I was dead chuffed. Thursday was the best day of the week, because Thursday was the day I got my benefits. One Thursday, when I'd lived in the flat for about four or five weeks, I remember cashing my book in the post office. I walked across the road to get a bus into town to do a bit of shopping. The bus stopped. It was really full but I got on and sat down. There was only my seat that was empty, except for a couple of other single seats. At the next stop, this guy got on. I was thinking, 'Oh no, I hope he doesn't sit next to me!' And I was just looking out of the window but he sat next to me and started chatting with me. He was really friendly, dead genuine. I remember getting off the bus and thinking, 'Wasn't that guy all right?' I remember thinking, 'What's he got that I've not got?'

As I said, that was on the Thursday.

Sunday, I was taking my little Jack Russell for a walk up Birch Road, past Birch Hill Hospital. It was quarter past twelve. I was walking up Birch Road with my dog and this group came walking down. As they got closer, I recognised one of them. It was the guy I met on the bus.

I stopped and said, 'Where've you been?'

He said, 'I've been to church.'

I thought, 'Oh no! He's a Bible basher. What's he going

to church for? Churches are for boring people, and older people, and those that have got nothing else better to do.' That's what I thought.

I said, 'That's cool.'

'Why don't you come along?'

'No way, mate. There's no getting me into church. I'm not into that.'

So he went his way and I went my way.

The next day I was walking my dog again up Birch Road, past Birch Hill Hospital. As I was walking past the hospital – because he told me the church was in the hospital grounds – I was kind of looking. I was looking for a church. I was looking for a cathedral. I was looking for the stained-glass windows. I was waiting to hear the bells. I was waiting to smell the smells. Have you got the picture of the graveyards? Because that's what churches are like, aren't they? But as I was walking, I was thinking, 'I can't see a church in the hospital grounds. They must have been having me on.'

The next day, as I did every day, I took my little dog, Kim, for a walk to these fields behind the hospital and as I was walking, I was thinking, 'I wonder where that church is?'

Well, remember I'd been in Cheadle Royal mental hospital. That was nine years before. I came out of Cheadle Royal and I'd been under loads of psychiatrists, but now that I'd moved to Rochdale, on the outskirts of Manchester, my records were being transferred from where I'd lived to where I'd moved to. You know, when you move house, your records follow you.

I had my first appointment with my new psychiatrist on a Wednesday. I walked into this psychiatric unit that was in the grounds of Birch Hill Hospital and an African guy was my psychiatrist – Dr Samuel Yangye. He had a nice suit on, nice quality glasses. He sat there really confident, in his chair. He got out my records and I had a bit of a chat with him, and I didn't think anything of it. He never said I couldn't get any of the drugs that I'd been getting. I thought, 'Fine.' I didn't think nowt of that.

That afternoon I was walking my dog, and as I was walking past this big hospital again, still I was thinking, 'I can't see that church.'

Friday morning, I was in my flat and there was a knock at my door. I opened it and there was this woman I'd never seen in my life. She said, 'Are you all right? I'm your next-door-but-one neighbour.'

I said, 'Are you?'

She said, 'I am. I've come to introduce myself. You've just moved up from Manchester, haven't you?'

'I have.'

'You used to be in a Salvation Army hostel, didn't you?'

'Yes.'

'Your dad drives a red car, doesn't he?'

I said, 'He does.'

She knew everything there was to know about me!

What?

Nosy neighbour.

I had a bit of a chat with her. Just before she left my doorstep I said, 'Dot?'

'What?'

'Can you do me a favour?'

'It depends what it is.'

I said, 'On Sunday I was walking up Birch Road, past Birch Hill Hospital, and I met a guy who says that he goes to church somewhere in the hospital grounds. Do you know where that church is, by any chance?'

'Oh, aye, love, I go to that church. I'll come and pick you up on Sunday morning.'

'No way! Church! No way.'

Sunday morning came and she picked me up. We walked up Birch Road together, into the hospital grounds, and she led me towards this building that had a sign outside that said, 'Doctor's Training Centre.' I thought, 'Where's she taking me? I thought she was taking me to church!' We walked through the foyer and at the side of the doctor's training centre there was a wooden prefab. There were about forty chairs out. I sat down on the second row, with my next-door neighbour. I was sat there thinking, 'What on earth am I doing here?' I was feeling really uncomfortable. 'What time is it going to be finished?'

Then, after being sat there for five minutes, there was a tap on my shoulder. I looked round and it was the guy that I'd met on the bus.

'What are you doing here?'

I said, 'Well, Dot . . .'

He said, 'I know Dot. She's my mate.'

'Well, she came for me. She brought me round.'

'It's great that you're here,' he said, and sat on the other side of me.

So now he was sat on one side with my next-door neighbour

on the other, and he'd got his wife and his tribe with him. I sat there thinking, 'What time is this going to be over? Church! What am I doing in church?'

Then, just before this service started, I heard from behind me, 'Hallelujah, praise the Lord.' I turned round and looked; it was my psychiatrist!

Remember I was suffering from an illness called amphetamine psychosis. I was hearing voices. I thought that people were following me. I am thinking, 'How did these guys know? How did they work it out to get me in here?' My psychiatrist was sitting directly behind me. Talk about pressure. I didn't know whether to rock and act daft or stand up straight. 'Come on, this guy is responsible for getting me my prescriptions! My psychiatrist is sat behind me. Oh no.'

Then the service started. It was a service that I will always remember because there was a guy on the front row who started to do a dance. Listen, I was into the nightclub scene, OK? I'm going to be honest, and this isn't blowing my own trumpet: in my heyday I could really cut a rug. I was a bit of a mover.

So here I was in this church and this guy started to do this dance. He was doing this Pentecostal two-step, or as Anglicans call it, 'The Resurrection Hop'. He was doing this dance up and down the front of the church, and I was thinking, 'What on earth is he doing? He wasn't even in time!' Music, dancing, and then Dot reached underneath her chair and pulled out a big tambourine. Tambourines! You didn't see many of them in the nightclubs. So my next-door neighbour was banging her tambourine, this guy was doing a dance, and my psychiatrist was sat behind me.

I looked round and Dr Yangye was really going. He was Pentecostal with a capital P. He was moving it big-time. 'That's my doctor! He's treating me. What chance have I got if he's my shrink?' He had a Bible underneath his arm, big enough to choke a donkey.

I was thinking, 'If people had told me church is this good, I'd have been here years ago. This is better than any LSD trip I've ever had.' Dancing, tambourine, my psychiatrist giving it this big-time. I was thinking, 'Wow!'

And then this guy got up to speak. At the end of the message he said this: 'We believe in a God who can heal. We want to pray for you if you've got any problems.'

Well, I believed there must be something out there. I never went to church, though. I had prayed a few crisis prayers, but that was it. From a kid I always believed there must be a God but that's as far as it got. Now this guy was telling me that God could heal me. He said, 'I want you to come and stand at the front.'

What had I got to lose? I was stood there, the only one, and I felt a right fool.

He came up to me and said, 'What can I pray with you for?'

I said, 'Well, I'm a heroin addict. I'm addicted to methadone. I've been hearing voices for the last nine years. I've got a constant fear in my stomach. Will you pray for me?'

'Yes. In the name of Jesus, we want to pray for this man's addictions. We want to pray for you to take away the fear from his stomach, and we pray for these voices.'

I thought, 'Don't tell them about the voices! They'll get worse.'

As he was praying for me, I remember this intense heat running from the top of my head to the soles of my feet. It was like a fire burning. I remember, like it was only last Sunday, shaking. I remember having goosebumps on the back of my neck as big as golf balls. I remember my hair being stood on end.

I remember crying, and where I come from, you don't cry.

But I was crying and I was thinking, 'Wow! What's all this about?'

He said, 'Amen.'

I opened my eyes and I walked back to where I'd been sat on that second row. There was a spring in my step. I had had an encounter with God and it revolutionised my life. The voices I'd heard for nine years disappeared.

Within four weeks I was off all the drugs.

I soon realised that God had a purpose for me. I went to work with an organisation called NET for one year and then I went off to Bible college.

In my last year at college I got busy setting up a charity, Proclaim Trust, to act as an administration base for the work that I was going to be doing.

See, for years my mission in life revolved around drugs. Now my mission in life is to make a difference in the lives of others.

CAN YOUR LIFE BE FIXED?
BY BARRY WOODWARD

I trust as you've read the stories in this book you've been inspired, intrigued and even challenged about your own situation.

It could be that as you've read *Fixed Lives* you've been thinking about the faith factor – the Christian faith that is the key factor to the change that has taken place in the lives of each person in this book.

It could be that you're asking the question, 'Will that work for me?' Yes, it will.

It might be that you've never found yourself caught up in a life of addiction, but you're still asking, 'Will the faith that these people have found work for me in my situation?' Well, the answer is 'yes'. See, the Christian faith is for everybody. Including you!

I always say there are two types of people who are part of the Christian church. There are those who can talk about what God has saved them from – that's the type of people who have been featured in the book – and we are the minority. Then there are those who can talk about what God has kept them from – that's those who have lived respectable lives – they are the majority. It doesn't matter which kind you are, because the Christian faith works for everyone. That means you!

Let me explain. The Bible is an instruction book. The letters B.I.B.L.E stand for Basic Instructions Before Leaving Earth! The Bible teaches us that there are faults, flaws and failures in all our lives. I know that you know that you are not perfect. None of us are; we have all made mistakes. It's this stuff in our lives that separates us from God because he is totally pure and holy. It creates a barrier. That's why Jesus came into the world. To sort this out so that we can make a connection with God.

Two thousand years ago, 2,000 miles away, God became a man – his name is Jesus. Jesus is God with skin on. And he came into this world and lived among the people of that time. He was tempted just like you and me, but he resisted temptation. Then at the age of thirty-three he was nailed to a cross. It was there that he paid the price for all your faults, flaws and failures. He did this so you can be forgiven. When we come to him and ask him for forgiveness, he wipes the slate clean. He gives us a brand new start!

My question to you is, though, 'Do you want one?' Do you want a brand new start in life? If you do, then you need to activate the Christian faith factor in your life. If you want to start a faith journey, the same one that people have talked about in Fixed Lives, then you can. This is what you need to do – you need to pray a simple prayer. The one below is a similar prayer to the one I prayed.

If you want to start that journey, pray this prayer out loud:

Dear God
I come to you today, and I admit that I need you. I ask that you forgive me for all my faults, for all my flaws and for all

my failures. Right now, I'm giving you consent to come into
my life. Give me a brand new start. And fix my life, like you
have with the people I've read about in this book.
I ask this in Jesus' name.
Amen.

Now you have prayed that prayer, you need to do the things
that all the people in this book did at the beginning of their
new faith factor journey.

First, you need to get a Bible (the Bible can also be found
in different versions on www.biblegateway.com). This is what
I did. The Bible is not one book that's to be read from front to
back like you would usually read a book. It's actually sixty-six
small books within one cover. It comes in two parts – Part 1
and Part 2 – or, the Old Testament and the New Testament.
Start by reading the book of John in the New Testament. You
could also find a Christian bookstore near to where you live
and ask them for some material to help you read your Bible.
Or you could Google 'Christian bookshops' in your area. Or
you could look online for things to help you read the Bible.
You will find that as you read it, God will speak to you, just
like he does with me.

Another thing you need to do is start to pray. I discovered
early on in my faith journey that this was one of the best
things I could do. Prayer is basically talking to God. When
we give God consent to come into our lives, it means that
from then on, he's there for us and he wants to be involved
with us, so he wants us to talk to him. You don't have to use
big fancy words when you pray; just be real and chat to God,

but remember who you are talking to! More than anything, God wants us to have a one-to-one with him. When we pray, that's what we are doing.

The third thing you need to do is find a Christian church. That's what we all did. God doesn't want us to go it alone. He wants us to make friends and come together and spend time worshipping him. That's why there are churches around. Don't just go to any church; it's important that you find one where the people believe that the Bible is true, and where Jesus is central to their teaching. When I started going to church I found that the people were there to help me if I needed it. You may even know someone who goes to church. Ask them to take you with them and introduce you to the minister.

You could also look at this website:

www.christianity.org.uk

Once you give God consent to come into your life and you do these three things, you will find out for yourself that the faith factor will work for you, just like it has done for all of us who have told our stories in *Fixed Lives*.

ABOUT PROCLAIM TRUST

HOPE • COMMUNICATION • INSPIRATION

Proclaim Trust is a registered charity. This non-profit making, interdenominational, organisation was established in 1999 to facilitate the work of Barry Woodward.

The primary function of Proclaim Trust is to inspirationally communicate the message of hope throughout the United Kingdom. The trust also equips people to engage in missional activities and mentors evangelists.

ABOUT BARRY WOODWARD

 Barry Woodward grew up in a great, non-Christian, home, in Salford, Greater Manchester. At 16, he left school with no qualifications and became drawn into the Manchester drugs scene, taking cannabis, amphetamines and LSD. This led to a life of heroin addiction and drug dealing.

After being dependent on heroin for fifteen years and spending a number of terms in prison, Barry had what he describes a 'religious experience', which resulted in his life being totally transformed. This led to him becoming an evangelist. Since then, he has worked with a number of Christian organizations and studied full time at Cliff College, where he was awarded a Diploma in Biblical Studies and Evangelistic Ministry from Sheffield University.

He is a contemporary communicator who is humourous, passionate and inspirational.

Each year, he speaks at approximately 130 events. He also occasionally contributes to discussions related to drug issues on the BBC, Channel 4 and Sky TV.

Barry is an accredited travelling minister with the Assemblies of God denomination, in the UK, and is also an associate evangelist with J.John of the Philo Trust. He is author of 'Once an Addict', and he and his wife Tina are members of the Bridge Church, Bolton, Greater Manchester.